THE GREAT REPUBLIC

PUTTING GOVERNMENT BACK IN ITS PROPER PLACE

John D. Blanton

THE GREAT REPUBLIC

Copyright © 2016 by John D. Blanton

World Ahead Press is a division of WND Books. The views and opinions expressed in this book are those of the author and do not necessarily reflect the official policy or position or WND Books.

Paperback ISBN: : 978-1-944212-10-0
eBook ISBN: 978-1-944212-11-7

Printed in the United States of America
16 17 18 19 20 21 LSI 9 8 7 6 5 4 3 2 1

CONTENTS

CHAPTER 1

A SORRY STATE OF AFFAIRS

"Power tends to corrupt, and absolute power corrupts absolutely."

JOHN EMERICH EDWARD DALBERG ACTON,
FIRST BARON ACTON (1834–1902)

What's wrong with the United States of America? Where do I even begin? I know. Lawlessness, where those responsible for enforcing the laws are not doing their duty.

Let me start with firearms. We have plenty of laws on the books, but are they being enforced? My answer is a resounding "no." They are not being enforced, or at the very least, they are not being enforced uniformly.

I find it funny, but not in an amusing way, that gun control is being pushed primarily by Democrats, because of the actions of a few crazed . . . Democrats. Most, but not all, of the recent mass murders were committed by people who the media identified as registered Democrats.

While the mass murders grab headlines, which the media loves to promote, most of the "gun violence" is actually committed by gangs. But they don't point the finger at the gangs. They point the finger at guns, as if guns are the problem. The real problem is gang violence. Compare the number of those killed in mass shootings to the number of people killed in one year in Chicago or Baltimore!

Another example of lawlessness is the so-called sanctuary cities, where enforcement of federal immigration laws is actually prohibited by local ordinances, with no repercussion from the federal government.

Then you have Colorado, where they passed a law permitting the possession and use of marijuana, in spite of the fact that the federal government has laws prohibiting such possession and use. Colorado is ignoring the federal laws. Neither of these two examples used the Nullification process to bypass federal law.

Next is the Defense of Marriage Act, signed into law by Bill Clinton, and ignored by Barack Obama. Article 2, Section 3 of the United States Constitution says that the president "...shall take Care that the Laws be faithfully executed . . ." It does not give the president permission to ignore a law with which he disagrees.

As for the Affordable Care Act, commonly known as Obamacare, the Supreme Court declared the FEE was a TAX, even when the writers said it was a fee and not a tax! And now we have to wait some more before the Supreme Court takes up the case challenging the Act on a violation of the Origination Clause.

Article 1, Section 7 of the United States Constitution says "All bills for raising Revenue shall originate in the House of Representatives; but the Senate may propose or concur with Amendments as on other Bills."

The Affordable Care Act would fail on the constitutionality check if the fee was declared a fee, so they called it a tax, but the Supreme Court didn't weigh in immediately. They should have struck it down on a violation of the Origination Clause, as the bill originated in the Senate, not the House, and not as an amendment to a bill. Why didn't they?

Barack Obama is ineligible to be President because he fails on the "Natural Born Citizen" clause - his father was not a US citizen at the time of his son's birth, but like most other laws, that one was ignored and downplayed.

Natural born citizen had a specific meaning at the time the Constitution of the United States was written. To get around that obstacle, the "powers that be" simply redefined the term to mean nothing more than "citizen." So now all that is required to become president is to either be born on United States territory or have one parent who was a citizen at the time of your birth! It is quite obvious that is not what the framers had in mind, otherwise they would have simply said "citizen" instead of the more specific "natural born citizen."

I also object to departments within the federal government that have grabbed more power simply by redefining terms. The Environmental Protection Agency has redefined "waterways" and "wetlands" in such a way that if it rains heavily and your back yard floods, your back yard is now considered a wetland and your next door neighbor, who has a new stream as the water finds a way out, now has a waterway in his yard! And now they can tell you what you can and can't do with your own property.

We are told that cigarettes are bad and have seen them banned from many places. New York is proposing a ban on smoking in private homes! They don't even like the e-cigarettes. But smoking marijuana is okay?

According to the American Lung Association, "Smoke from marijuana combustion has been shown to contain many of the same toxins, irritants and carcinogens as tobacco smoke."

Why is smoking cigarettes bad and smoking marijuana is okay? My theory is that it has everything to do with "big tobacco" - companies that sell cigarettes. There are no companies selling marijuana. No companies making "huge profits" that they can go after.

Why does the government go after "big oil"? Because the product is dirty, smelly, pollutes the air, and, worst of all, the companies that find it, pump it, refine it, and sell it, making "huge profits" from it. It doesn't matter that the United States government, in the form of taxation, makes more money from gasoline than the companies that sell it!

Governments are now trying to tell us what we can and cannot consume, especially in New York. They banned trans-fats. They banned smoking. They banned soft drinks in containers larger than, what, twenty ounces? Who are they to tell us what we can and can't consume? They want to protect our health? Why? Oh, because they are paying for our health care? Because of Obamacare?

The government has done such a bang-up job with the Post Office, which is running billions of dollars in debt each year, that they want to expand into our health care? Yes, the government will do a great job with that, too.

Just look at the War on Poverty! Wait, that's not won, yet? It's been going on for fifty years! And how many trillions of dollars has been spent on it? What about the war on terror? No, that one hasn't been won, either!

And as for illegal immigration, the Food and Drug Administration can track every cow in the United States, but customs and border patrol can't find all the illegal immigrants? Give me a break! It isn't racist to expect our laws to be followed and enforced! People come here illegally from all continents in the world, except Antarctica!

What is wrong with some people? They defend illegal immigration by saying that this is a nation of immigrants! Yes! But LAWFUL immigrants! Immigrants who came to live and stay! To become AMERICANS! They were not coming here to make money to send home, like so many do now. These same illegal immigrants vote in their own nations' elections! They are FOREIGN NATIONALS, living in the United States ILLEGALLY.

These same people who defend illegal immigration also want open borders, or better yet, no borders. With no borders, you have no country. Why don't Mexico,

Canada, Great Britain, China, Russia, Germany, et al, open their borders? Why not do away with visas and passports? Nobody else will do that because they know that is the fastest way to lose their country.

Here, if we open the borders to everyone, who knows who will come across. More people who want to fly planes into buildings? More people who want to cut other people's heads off? Or people who want to change this country from a constitutional republic to a dictatorship?

There are already those who want to give illegal immigrants the right to vote, especially in local elections, "because they live here, too." Giving them the right to vote is akin to giving them citizenship. I believe that if you want to vote, you must be a citizen, otherwise, what's the point?

As I see it, illegal immigrants are showing no respect for this country by coming here without permission. They may also be the same people who are "offended" by the American flag and American patriotism. Now, American students, in the United States, cannot come to school showing national pride and they are also being taught that this nation has done nothing worth being proud of.

Textbooks, like Howard Zinn's *A People's History of the United States*, show off a lot of the bad things that were done in this country's history, ignoring the worse things that other countries have done, and ignoring the good that we have done, all for the sake of his ideology. His book would not have "sold millions" if schools and universities hadn't mandated that students purchase it for their curriculum!

Whatever happened to "America, the Melting Pot?" It has now become the Balkanization of America, where groups are segregating themselves, not integrating. I am not saying that this nation is, or was, without its problems, but showing the bad and little of the good, for the sake of "historical honesty" does not promote unity. It promotes the reverse, where groups find other groups to "blame for their problems."

Toward the back of Zinn's book, he discussed the 2000 presidential election, and how the Republicans "manipulated" the events in Florida to give the election to George W. Bush. He left out the rest of the story in order to paint the Republicans as the "bad guys" who stole the election.

He didn't tell his readers that the courts stopped the recounts because it was violating the equal protection clause, that the recounts were only taking place in certain counties, not state-wide as the law directed. He didn't tell his readers that after the election was decided, the media and others continued with an "unofficial" recount and that each recount resulted in the same thing - that George W. Bush won. He didn't tell his readers that he and his like-minded associates were angry that Gore won the popular vote but lost the electoral vote.

Another grievance I have with the media is that with the election of Barack Obama, they expounded every chance they got that the only reason people opposed him was because of his skin color. They cried "racism" every time someone opposed his ideas. To them, it had nothing to do with political ideology, as if everyone believed the same way they did and were opposing the president simply because he was black. Never mind that Obama is half white, and the other half is split between Arab and black. I couldn't care less about his skin color.

What does the color of one's skin have to do with a person's mind, heart, ideas and values? Why skin color? Why not associate eye color with intelligence? Hair color with compassion? The attachment, or not, of earlobes to wealth?

What really got me started on this project was that every day I would turn on the television and watch the news and see what Congress and the president were up to. I read the newspapers and news on the internet and it was always the same: The scandals, the denials of scandals, the lies, the cheating. The manipulation.

I got so fed up that I started to take notes on how to plug the loopholes those in government were using. And then the notes started to pile up. My initial idea was to create amendments to the Constitution, but after seeing how many notes were in the stack, there was only one thing left to do. I re-wrote the Constitution! It was not done lightly or on a whim but with some very serious thought.

After a while, it got to the point of how to share these thoughts with others. And so this book was born. Hopefully, you will see in this book just how far our politicians have taken us. It is not a "call to arms." Not by a long shot. This is intended to get people thinking about what is going on and how to give this great country a proper course correction.

I do have some explaining to do, such as why I wrote the Constitution of the Great Republic, and why I gave it that name.

Well, first, the name came about because of Franklin Delano Roosevelt and George W. Bush. It was under FDR that the United States was to be the "Arsenal of Democracy" and George W. Bush frequently spoke of spreading "democracy".

How strange. The United States of America is not a democracy but a republic. Nowhere in the Constitution does it mention "democracy" but it does say "republic." Also, in the Pledge of Allegiance, there is the phrase "and to the Republic, for which it stands." Why do people always refer to the United States as a Democracy? Someone once said that, "a Democracy is two wolves and a lamb voting on what to have for lunch." Therefore, I decided to remove all doubt and call the new nation the Great Republic. That way, no one could say it was a democracy.

The other reason for calling it the Great Republic is that I wanted to remove all geographical and ethnic attachments, such as the United States of **America.** The Constitution of the Great Republic allows the possible expansion of the country to other parts of the globe and I did not want those who may want to join later to feel left out. The goal was to ultimately be a world government of the people, by the people, and for the people.

Please keep in mind that membership in the Great Republic is strictly voluntary. No state should be forced to join or forced to stay, but that is another matter entirely and will be dealt with later.

And for those, like me, who liked the rest of the previous quote . . . "Democracy is two wolves and a lamb voting on what to have for lunch. **Liberty is a well-armed lamb contesting the vote.**" I wonder now if this is the true reason for some people's desire for disarming law-abiding citizens.

Now, why did I write the Constitution of the Great Republic? It actually started in my mind prior to 2007. There were things going on in politics that I did not agree with, such as a lack of congressional term limits. Apparently, no one in Congress wanted term limits, even though the idea was gaining ground with the people.

For members of Congress, the Constitution of the United States would have to be amended "over their dead bodies" as the saying goes. Those in Congress hold power and are loath to give any of it up. Why should they when there are so many perks and so much money to be had? They frequently give themselves raises and seem to be looking to tax anything and everything. As Reagan said of government, "If it moves, tax it. If it keeps moving, regulate it. And if it stops moving, subsidize it."

The more news I read and saw, the less I liked what was going on in Washington, D.C. For one thing, there were George W. Bush's "signing statements" where he said how he "interpreted" the law and what parts he would enforce. For another, there was *Kelo v. the City of New London* where they re-interpreted Eminent

Domain. And don't get me started on the Patriot Act. That one was wrong on so many levels!

Then, starting in 2008, there was the flap over Barack Obama's birth certificate and how nobody seemed to have any legal "standing" with the courts to demand he prove his eligibility, in addition to the definition of natural born citizen being re-defined to mean you had only to be born on United States soil, that the citizenship of your parents was irrelevant.

There was also congressman John Shadegg of Arizona, who proposed the Enumerated Powers Act (HR 450) that apparently Congress still does not want to pass. The Act would "require Congress to specify the source of authority under the United States Constitution for the enactment of laws, and for other purposes." Apparently Congress does not want to tell us by what authority they are considering or passing bills.

Then there's corruption. I was tired of the same old system where corrupt politicians have gotten into power and become entrenched. It had nothing to do with "Democrats" or "Republicans" but had everything to do with limiting the power of government and reducing the damage corrupt politicians can cause. I have since concluded that those in power do not wish to give up their power and are unlikely, in the extreme, to ever let any of these ideas for true reform come up for a vote.

The origin of this book started as ideas written on scraps of paper. Every time these people in Congress did something I felt they had no right to do, I added another scrap to my collection. Finally, I decided to put them in the computer, to store them all in one place.

I shared my ideas with a chancellor at a university on the East Coast, who suggested it would be easier to implement them if they were made into amendments to the Constitution. But as more time progressed, the more I read and saw, the more ideas that came to mind, the holes that needed plugging, I felt that so many changes were needed that it would require too many amendments, and since I had no faith that even one of them would ever be allowed to even come up for a vote, I decided to re-write the entire Constitution as a form of therapy. Actually, it might be better to say I re-edited the Constitution because I took the original, added in all the amendments, added in my notes, removed portions of text and re-arranged the order of the Articles.

I have to admit that I did look at the Constitution of the Confederate States of America. To be honest, I found it appallingly horrible and I'm glad it didn't stand. I also examined the Articles of Confederation, our first form of government, and found it to be just as bad. At no point did I look at constitutions of other nations. I kept it in-house, so to speak.

As I re-wrote the Constitution of the United States of America, it gave me a good understanding of the rights and powers of government, the states and the people. It also gave me a profound appreciation for what the original writers did. For one thing, they did not have computers to correct errors and fine tune their work. For another, commuting from New York to Boston, or New York to Philadelphia, was not nearly as fast or easy as it is today.

There may be some people who will try to charge me with plagiarizing the Constitution of the United States. My response to that is I took ideas from the best source available! But in reality, it would be plagiarism only if I passed it off as my own work. Keep in mind that the writers of the Constitution of the United States could also be accused of plagiarism because many of the ideas they incorporated into their document came from other sources as well. They can't be accused because they didn't claim credit either. Now, plagiarism aside, at this point my project was going to be called the Second Constitution of the United States of America. And then Congress did something stupid.

When they passed the second stimulus bill in January of 2009, plus all the other spending bills, putting the taxpayers of the United States further into debt, I decided to make a clean break. The members of Congress and the President of the United States, in "my" name, as a taxpayer and constituent, were piling on the debt. A debt that our grandchildren would be obligated to pay. A debt that probably would never be paid because, by pushing a socialist agenda, Congress would drive companies out of business. An example is the state of Michigan. They tax businesses so much that they are leaving the state. Detroit is a shadow of what it once was. So, by creating the Great Republic, I would free myself and others from the debt of the United States of America. Any state wishing to join could do so and those states wishing to stay with the United States could then carry the burden of debt Congress has so graciously given them.

When re-writing the Constitution, and giving rise to a new country, I had several advantages. First, there was no personal, moral, or political opposition - no issues of slavery that the original writers were confronted with, and no special interest groups trying to bully or bribe their way into getting special treatment. The Constitution of the United States, brilliant as it was, was still hampered by special interests. They had to compromise in order to get it passed, including allowing slavery to continue. I learned from the successes and failures of the past and incorporated them into the future.

As a solitary writer, I could be concise and uniform throughout the document and put in it whatever I wanted. And so I did. I kept in mind the possibility that the new constitution could be manipulated and abused and I have tried to protect against that. I did not put anything in that would give me or my family any advantage over others. The whole purpose and goal was to do what was right, not what was expedient, and to eliminate as much corruption as possible by taking away the power of the political elite, the wealthy elite, the union elite, and the corporate elite and put it back into the hands of We the People, for the People. The Elites have come to feel that they know what is best for us, when they are only people, just as we are.

In the end, I was right about one thing. It would not have been practical to turn these changes into amendments. I would have needed to create roughly ninety amendments to cover everything that I changed!

I have no illusions that this will EVER come to pass, but putting it down on paper was therapy for me, especially with what Congress was doing at the time—trying to pass the health care bill in spite of the fact that the majority of Americans and nearly all the Republicans in Congress were opposed to it. Nancy Pelosi didn't help either, saying, "We have to pass it in order to read it."

She was right, in her own way. Much of the language hadn't been written at the time and she knew that it was going to be written not by members of Congress but by bureaucrats, that Congress wasn't going to vote on any of the provisions, only that they were going to vote on the basic framework. I doubt if many read it even after it was passed.

There is a lesson to be learned from history: My understanding is that corrupt people always try to gain positions of power, and then use that power for personal gain, and to keep their power. Some fine examples are New York City's Tammany Hall and the Teapot Dome Scandal!

Some people want power over others and do not care who gets hurt as they strive to attain it. Examples include Hugo Chavez, Fidel Castro, Pol Pot, Mao Zedong, Adolf Hitler, Idi Amin, and Kim Jong Il. When George Washington stepped down after two terms as president, many people, including the King of England, were stunned. Here was a man who had power and could have held onto it much longer and he let it go. It was a very profound act at that time, and our current system of succession still is.

Then there are some countries that have a revolution to throw off a tyrannical government only to fall into another tyrannical government. Fidel Castro comes to mind. He overthrew a dictator and became one himself. Hugo Chavez didn't want to let go of power and changed Venezuela's Constitution in order to keep it. And how many times has the government of Bolivia been overthrown in their history? Over a hundred?

These people all want (or wanted) power over others, to control others, to be feared, admired, or worshiped by others. And the desire for wealth should not be overlooked, either. These people are/were ruthless and cruel, especially towards those who don't fall in line, who criticized them. Such were the kings of old.

These people were also aided by those who wanted to be "on the winning side," or who were allowed by their masters to be as cruel as they wanted, or who also wanted power and control over others. Some became members of the new government while others became members of secret police or death squads. Che Guevara was one of those violent and ruthless brutes, not a brave and noble revolutionary as he is imagined to be by some.

Many dictators were voted into power and took advantage of a crisis, manufactured or otherwise, to propel themselves further than their constitutions allowed. Julius Cesar and Adolph Hitler were guilty of this.

I wanted to limit the number of corrupt people entering into government positions, to remove the temptation, and ability, of those in government to become corrupt, and to promote liberty.

In 2009, I sent earlier versions of my re-written Constitution to others. One was sent to someone in the Libertarian Party, another was to a chancellor at a university. I even showed it to my friends and co-workers. I felt that now was the time to share it with the world.

Very recently, there have been people throwing out the word "secession." I heard it coming from New Hampshire, Vermont, Connecticut, and Texas, to name but a few states that mentioned it. Part of me felt that if there were a real secession movement, I would rather have something in place just in case it happened.

I read online how secession is "illegal" and just plain wrong. I asked people where, in the United States Constitution, that it said secession is illegal. They had no answer, but insisted it was, and that the Civil War settled the issue. The answer, in reality, is that secession is NOT unconstitutional. The Constitution does not mention it, therefore it remains as a power to the states or to the people. Just because secessionists lost in the Civil War does not make it illegal.

I believe that the states could peacefully secede, but only if the federal government did nothing to stop them. It gets messy when the federal government decides to use force to prevent secession. In doing so, it tells the people that they are not in fact, free citizens, but are subjects. Subjects are not allowed to leave. Sure, the government doesn't care if a few people here or there change their citizenship status, but for masses of people, they cannot permit it.

Some people might say that this book and Constitution constitutes treason against the United States of America. I would vehemently disagree. I believe that many members of our government have betrayed our country far beyond what I could do with this project.

I want people to come away from this book with ideas about what needs to be changed in our country and in the Constitution of the United States. I would also point out that the Revolution itself, by the standards being bandied about today, would have been considered "illegal" and "unconstitutional."

I know there will be those who are opposed to the ideas in this book, and some have legitimate concerns. Others are more selfish. One legitimate concern is what happens to those currently living on Social Security and other entitlement programs. There are a lot of people who have paid into Social Security and Medicare and have not begun to use them. Will they lose their benefits?

At the current rate of spending, Social Security won't be around much longer anyway. Congress has been treating it as its own little piggy bank. Whenever they need money, they borrow from Social Security. They seem to borrow more than they pay back and the longer we live the more people will be on it and fewer paying into it so eventually it will run out.

I suspect that is one of the reasons for the Affordable Care Act. What it will accomplish would be the reduction of doctors, leading to rationed care, especially for the elderly. It would save the government a lot of money (in Social Security, Medicare and Medicaid) if more elderly died. For me, I want my money back and I'll decide how and where to invest it (or spend it foolishly as I see fit).

As for Medicare, it is currently paying out more than it is bringing in. In the real world, that would result in eventual bankruptcy. These programs aren't going to be around much longer unless some drastic and draconian changes are made. Raising taxes is not the answer, as it actually reduces revenues instead of increasing them, because people would have less money to spend.

Under the new Constitution, people in general, state governments, and small businesses stand the most to gain. Those who stand the most to lose would be certain members of Congress, large corporations who have grown fat on government contracts, and those wanting advantages over others. These people will lose a lot of power under the new Constitution.

Those in Congress won't be able to continue to run for office until they die, and they won't be able to give themselves raises, just to name but a few of the changes. Certain corporations and unions will also find their power and influence sharply limited. The new Constitution will be a government of the people, not unions and corporations.

Socialists and Communists would also lose out under the new Constitution. Finally, those who are currently living on welfare and other social programs, when they are fully capable of supporting themselves with real jobs, and illegal immigrants, would most likely also be opposed to this new Constitution.

Welfare, food stamps, and other entitlement programs will also be affected. This Constitution does not mandate any of these social programs. In fact, it prohibits the government from contributing to them. If people want to contribute funds to keep them going, as charities, they may. Charities, in my opinion, can be held more accountable than our own government! So far as I know, no one has gone to jail over the fraud and abuse in Social Security and Medicare programs.

In the early 1900s people looked after each other. If given the chance, I believe they still will. We should not be depending on the government in order to survive. When we depend on government to survive, then they can tell us what we can eat, what we can drive, where we can live. We stop being citizens and become subjects (slaves). The government can encourage charities to pick up the slack on these programs, with voluntary donations by the people.

If you give government power, then you better be prepared for the consequences. If the government can dictate a minimum wage, then it also stands to reason that it can dictate a maximum wage.

As I see it, at the rate things are going, the people of the United States shall be ruled not by the Constitution, but by bureaucracies. The EPA, and so many other government departments, are passing rules that affect The People. These are unelected people with no accountability to government, with rules passed not by representatives in Congress but by bureaucratic committees.

And what about the agencies that are sued and then settle out of court in order to establish a "requirement" for "new regulations?" That is not how the system is supposed to work.

No accountability? Yes. That's right. No accountability. Just look at the Federal Reserve! Congress established it in 1913 and yet today, their books cannot be examined! The Federal Reserve dictates, yes, dictates, how much the interest rates are each year. They make loans and do not disclose who they are to, or when they will be paid back. If they are doing nothing wrong, then why are they preventing Congress, which has the Constitutional requirements regarding money, from examining their records?

As for the Federal Reserve, they are keeping the interest rates low so that the trillions of dollars of debt can be managed more easily, but if they decide to raise interest rates, then the United States would have to pay more in interest on that debt. I think they are manipulating it for political reasons, one of which is to keep the man in the Oval Office from looking bad.

So, no accountability, the rule by bureaucratic fiat, staggering debt, and the unequal enforcement of the laws. This truly is a sorry state of affairs.

CHAPTER 2

THE CONSTITUTION
OF THE GREAT REPUBLIC

We hold these truths to be self-evident, that all people are created equal, that they are endowed by their Creator with certain unalienable Rights, that among these are Life, Liberty and the pursuit of Happiness, and that the Government of the Great Republic derives its just powers from the consent of the governed.

ARTICLE 1

SECTION 1

The executive Power shall be vested in a President of the Great Republic. The President shall hold the Office during the Term of Four Years, and, together with the Vice-President, chosen for the same Term, be elected as follows: A candidate shall receive one Electoral Point for every Congressional District they shall win by popular vote within said District. The candidate who receives the most Electoral Points shall be declared the winner of the election. In the event of a tie, the candidate with the most popular votes nationwide shall be declared the winner.

No person except a Natural Born Citizen shall be eligible to the Office of President or Vice President; neither shall any Person be eligible to that Office who shall not have attained the Age of thirty-five Years, and been fourteen Years a Resident within the Great Republic.

No person shall be elected to the Office of the President more than twice, and no person who has held the Office of President, or acted as President, for more than two years of a term to which some other person was elected President shall be elected to the Office of the President more than once.

In Case of the Removal of the President from Office, or of his or her Death, Resignation, or Inability to discharge the Powers and Duties of the said Office, the same shall devolve on the Vice President, and the Congress may by Law provide for the Case of Removal, Death, Resignation or Inability, both of the President and Vice President, declaring what Officer shall then act as President, and such Officer shall act accordingly, until the Disability be removed, or a President shall be elected.

The President shall, at stated Times, receive for his Services, a Compensation, which shall neither be increased nor diminished during the

Period for which he shall have been elected, and he shall not receive within that Period any other Emolument from the Great Republic, or the States thereof.

Before he enter on the Execution of his Office, he shall take the following Oath or Affirmation: 'I do solemnly swear (or affirm) that I will faithfully execute the Office of President of the Great Republic, and will to the best of my ability, preserve, protect and defend the Constitution of the Great Republic.'

SECTION 2

The President shall be Commander in Chief of the Armed Forces of the Great Republic, and of the Militia of the several States when called into the actual Service of the Great Republic; the President may require the Opinion, in writing, of the principal Officer in each of the executive Departments, upon any subject relating to the Duties of their respective Offices.

He shall have Power, by and with the Advice and Consent of the Congress, to make Treaties, provided three-fifths in each House concur; and he shall nominate, and by and with the Consent of Congress, shall appoint Ambassadors, other public Ministers and Consuls, and all other Officers of the Great Republic, whose Appointments are not herein otherwise provided for, and which shall be established by Law.

SECTION 3

He shall from time to time give to the Congress Information of the State of the Union, and recommend to their Consideration such Measures as he shall judge necessary and expedient; he may, on extraordinary Occasions, convene both Houses, or either of them; he shall receive Ambassadors and other public Ministers; he shall take Care that the Laws be faithfully executed, and shall Commission all the Officers of the Great Republic.

SECTION 4

The President, Vice President and all civil Officers of the Great Republic, shall be removed from Office on Impeachment for, and Conviction of, Treason, Bribery, or other high Crimes and Misdemeanors. Trial of Impeachment resides in the Senate and Judgment of Impeachment resides in the House of Representatives.

SECTION 5

If it is found that either the President or Vice President shall be ineligible for the Office after they have been sworn in and taken the title and mantle of President or Vice President, they shall both be considered ineligible and immediately removed from Office as they were both elected together; all of their Acts while in Office shall be made Null and Void; and the Candidates that came in second in the election shall be sworn in and serve the remainder of the term.

Any Bill passed by Congress and signed into Law, or vetoed by the ineligible President but not over-ridden by Congress, shall be presented to the new President, after being sworn into Office, as if it had just been passed by Congress. Any Bill passed by Congress that was vetoed by the ineligible President but over-ridden by Congress shall stand.

SECTION 6

In case of the removal of the President from office or of his death or resignation, or if the President elect should die before being sworn into office, the Vice President shall become President.

Whenever there is a vacancy in the office of the Vice President, the President shall nominate a Vice President who shall take office upon confirmation by a majority vote of both Houses of Congress.

Whenever the President transmits to the President Pro Tempore of the Senate and the Speaker of the House of Representatives his written declaration that he is unable to discharge the powers and duties of his office, and until he transmits to them a written declaration to the contrary, such powers and duties shall be discharged by the Vice President as Acting President.

Whenever the Vice President and a majority of either the principal officers of the executive departments or of such other body as Congress may by law provide, transmit to the President Pro Tempore of the Senate and the Speaker of the House of Representatives their written declaration that the President is unable to discharge the powers and duties of his office, the Vice President shall immediately assume the powers and duties of the office as Acting President.

Thereafter, when the President transmits to the President Pro Tempore of the Senate and the Speaker of the House of Representatives his written declaration that no inability exists, he shall resume the powers and duties of his office unless the Vice President and a majority of either the principal officers of the executive department or of such other body as Congress may by law provide, transmit within four days to the President Pro Tempore of the Senate and the Speaker of the House of Representatives their written declaration that the President is unable to discharge the powers and duties of his office. Thereupon Congress shall decide the issue, assembling within forty eight hours for that purpose if not in session. If the Congress, within twenty one days after receipt of the latter written declaration, or, if Congress is not in session, within twenty one days after Congress is required to assemble, determines by three-fifths vote of both Houses that the President is unable to discharge the powers and duties of his office, the Vice President shall continue to discharge the same as Acting President; otherwise, the President shall resume the powers and duties of his office.

If there is a vacancy in the office of the President and Vice President at the same time, other than ineligibility, then the following Office-holders, in order, shall become President and serve out the remainder of the term: Speaker of the House, President Pro Tempore of the Senate, Secretary of State, Secretary of the Treasury, Secretary of War, and the Attorney General, as head of the Justice Department.

SECTION 7

The President shall have the power to veto specific provisions of any Appropriation Bill without vetoing the entire bill. Such specific vetoes are subject to override by Congress.

SECTION 8

The President shall not issue any Executive Order that violates the law or the Constitution, or requires expenditure or prevents expenditure of taxpayer funds, or modifies or alters a Law or alters how a Law is implemented or enforced.

The Supreme Court has the authority to review Executive Orders. Executive Orders deemed by the Supreme Court to be in violation of the Constitution shall be rendered Null and Void.

SECTION 9

The President shall have Power, by and with the Consent of the Senate, to appoint the principal Officer for the four Executive Departments; the Executive Departments being Justice, State, Treasury, and War. Each Officer shall be appointed, provided three-fifths of Congress concurs. No additional Executive Departments shall be created.

All rules, regulations, guidelines, and doctrines of any Agency or Department in the Federal Government must be passed by Congress and signed into Law by the President. The Great Republic shall not be ruled by Bureaucracy.

No Department or Agency of the Federal Government shall be self-funding or have independent means of financing their operations; All funding shall come from Congress.

SECTION 10

The President shall have the Power to use the Armed Forces to protect the People and Interests of the Great Republic for up to fourteen consecutive days without the consent of Congress, during which time Congress shall vote for or against a Declaration of War. Prior to or upon the commencement of the use of force, the President shall give notice to Congress of said action. If Congress shall vote against a Declaration of War, the Armed Forces shall be ordered to withdraw and cease hostilities immediately. Invasion of the territory of the Great Republic by outside forces constitutes an automatic Declaration of War.

ARTICLE 2

SECTION 1

All legislative Powers herein granted shall be vested in a Congress of the Great Republic, which shall consist of a Senate and House of Representatives.

The Congress shall assemble at least once in every year, and such meeting shall begin at noon on the 2nd day of January.

SECTION 2

The House of Representatives shall be composed of Members chosen every second Year by the People in their District of their State; and each Representative shall have one Vote. Representatives are the voice of the People of their State in Congress.

A Candidate for Representative must have attained the Age of twenty-five Years and been a Citizen of the Great Republic for a minimum of seven years, or a Citizen of the Great Republic at the time of the Adoption of this Constitution, and must be an Inhabitant of the State in which the Candidate is seeking office for no less than two years prior to the election.

Representatives shall be apportioned among the several States which may be included within this Union, according to their respective Numbers. The Number of Representatives shall be one for every Six Hundred Thousand, but each State shall have at Least one Representative.

When vacancies happen in the Representation from a State, the Legislature of that State shall fill such vacancy until the next election.

No person shall serve more than six years in the House of Representatives, with no more than two years in leadership.

The House of Representatives shall choose their Speaker and other Officers; and shall have the sole Power of Judgment in Cases of Impeachment.

Judgment in Cases of Impeachment shall not extend further than removal from Office, and disqualification to hold and enjoy any Office of honor, Trust or Profit under the Great Republic; but the Party convicted shall nevertheless be liable and subject to Indictment, Trial, Judgment and Punishment, according to Law. No Person shall be removed from Office without the Concurrence of two-thirds of the Members present.

SECTION 3

The Senate shall be composed of three Senators from each State, chosen by the Legislature of the several States; and each Senator shall have one Vote. Senators are the voice of their State in Congress.

A Candidate for Senate must have attained the Age of thirty Years and been a Citizen of the Great Republic for a minimum of nine years, or a Citizen of the Great Republic at the time of the Adoption of this Constitution, and must be an Inhabitant of the State in which the Candidate is seeking office for no less than six years prior to the election.

When vacancies happen in the Representation from a State, the Legislature of that State shall fill such vacancy until the next election.

Immediately after they shall be assembled in Consequence of the first Election, they shall be divided as equally as may be into three Classes. The Seats of the Senators of the first Class shall be vacated at the Expiration of the second Year, of the second Class at the Expiration of the fourth Year, and of the third Class at the Expiration of the sixth Year, so that one third may be chosen every second Year.

No person shall be elected to the Senate more than once. No person who has held the office of Senator for more than two years of a term to which another person was elected Senator shall be eligible to serve in the Senate again. No person shall serve more than eight years in the Senate, with no more than two years in leadership.

The Vice President of the Great Republic shall be President of the Senate, but shall have no

Vote, unless they be equally divided.

The Senate shall choose their other Officers, and also a President Pro Tempore, in the absence of the Vice President, or when he shall exercise the Office of President of the Great Republic.

The Senate shall have the sole Power to try all Impeachments. When sitting for that Purpose, they shall be on Oath or Affirmation. When the President of the Great Republic is tried, the Chief Justice shall preside. And no Person shall be convicted without the Concurrence of two-thirds of the Members present.

SECTION 4

The Places and Manner of holding Elections for Senators and Representatives, outside of what is prescribed in this Constitution, shall be prescribed in each State by the Legislature thereof.

Each House shall be the Judge of the Elections, Returns and Qualifications of its own Members, and a Majority of each shall constitute a Quorum to do Business; but a smaller number may adjourn from day to day, and may be authorized to compel the Attendance of absent Members, in such Manner, and under such Penalties as each House may provide.

Each House may determine the Rules of its Proceedings, punish its Members for disorderly Behavior, and, with the Concurrence of two-thirds, expel a Member.

Each House must determine the Rules of its Proceedings within the first week of meeting; such Rules shall not be subject to change until the next Congress is elected.

Each House shall keep a Journal of its Proceedings, and publish the same weekly, excepting such Parts as may in their Judgment require Secrecy; and the Yeas and Nays of the Members of either House on any question shall be entered on the Journal. No vote shall be conducted by a Show of Hands or by Voice.

Neither House, during the Session of Congress, shall, without the Consent of the other, adjourn for more than three days, nor to any other Place than that in which the two Houses shall be sitting.

SECTION 5

The Senators and Representatives shall in all Cases, except Treason, Felony and Breach of the Peace, be privileged from Arrest during their Attendance at the Session of their respective Houses, and in going to and returning from the same; and for any Speech or Debate in either House, they shall not be questioned in any other Place.

No member of Congress shall be exempt from paying fines and fees, including but not limited to speeding tickets, parking violations and overdraft charges.

No Senator or Representative shall, during the Time for which he was elected, be appointed to any civil Office under the Authority of the Great Republic which shall have been created, or the Emoluments whereof shall have been increased during such time; and no Person holding any other Office under the Great Republic, shall be a Member of either House during his Continuance in Office.

SECTION 6

Every Bill, Order, or Resolution coming before each House must be passed by three-fifths of that House in order to pass, with the exception of Bills to repeal a previously passed Law.

A Bill to repeal a previously passed Law must be passed by a Simple Majority of each House and does not require the President's signature. No Law shall be exempt from being repealed.

Bills from each House must be unified by Conference Committee and sent back to each House for final Passage by the same ratios as above.

Every Bill which shall have passed the House of Representatives and the Senate, shall, before it becomes a Law, be presented to the President of the Great Republic; If he approves he shall sign it, but if not he shall return it, with his Objections to that House in which it shall have originated, who shall enter the Objections at large on their Journal, and proceed to reconsider it. If after such Reconsideration two-thirds of that House shall agree to pass the Bill, it shall be sent, together with the Objections, to the other House, by which it shall likewise be reconsidered, and if approved by two-thirds of that House, it shall become a Law. But in all such Cases the Votes of both Houses shall be determined by Yeas and Nays, and the Names of the Persons voting for and against the Bill shall be entered on the Journal of each House respectively. At no time shall a Vote be held by a Show of Hands or by Voice.

If any Bill shall not be returned by the President within twenty-one days after it shall have been presented to him, the Same shall be returned as if he Objected to it and shall not become a Law, subject to Reconsideration.

Every Bill shall be limited to one Subject with no Riders, Amendments, or other Attachments, and shall be Limited to a maximum of fifty standard letter size pages, single spaced with a twelve point font and a line height of 0.18 of an inch, and with one inch margins. No Bill shall reference another Document in order to circumvent said limitations.

Every Bill shall be made available to the public for reading seventy-two hours prior to being voted upon. Each member of Congress must indicate under oath that they have read the Bill before voting on it.

All bills for Taxation and raising Revenue shall originate in the House of Representatives.

SECTION 7

The Congress shall have the following Enumerated Powers:

To lay and collect a tax on all goods sold by corporations and organizations without apportionment among the several States, and without regard to any census or enumeration; goods being defined as physical, tangible items; currency, electronic data, and services shall not be considered goods; the only acceptable form of taxation on real property is on the sale or transfer from one owner to another; no tax shall be levied by calling it another name, such as a "fee", "permit", or "license"; the maximum tax rate shall not be more than Ten Percent;

To borrow money on the credit of the Great Republic only during the time of a Declared War, but shall be prohibited from borrowing from foreign creditors, and the monies borrowed must be used pursuant to said War;

To establish a uniform Rule of Naturalization and Immigration, and uniform Laws on the subject of Bankruptcies throughout the Great Republic;

To coin Money, regulate the Value thereof, and of foreign Coin, and fix the Standard of Weights and Measures; Congress shall not delegate this authority; the Monetary System of the Great Republic shall be based solely on the Gold Standard; The currency of the Great Republic shall be known as the Republic Dollar;

To provide for the Punishment of counterfeiting the Securities and Coin of the Great Republic;

To promote the Progress of Science, by securing for thirty years to Authors and Inventors the exclusive Right to their respective Writings and Discoveries;

To constitute Tribunals inferior to the Supreme Court;

To define and punish Piracies and Felonies committed on the high Seas, and Offenses against the Law of Nations;

To Declare War, provided seventy percent in each House concurs, grant Letters of Marque and Reprisal, and make Rules concerning Captures on Land, Water, Air and Space;

To raise, support, and maintain the Armed Forces; The Armed Forces of the Great Republic, known as the Republic Marines, shall be composed of one Branch, with one uniform and one rank system; Service in the Armed Forces shall be strictly voluntary; Only Citizens may serve in the Armed Forces;

To make Rules for the Government and Regulation of the Armed Forces; Congress shall not delegate this authority;

To provide for calling forth the Militia to suppress Insurrections and repel Invasions; the Militia being all able-bodied citizens, regardless of gender, between the ages of Twenty-five and Forty and considered by law eligible for military service;

To provide for organizing, arming, and disciplining the Militia, and for governing such Part of them as may be employed in the Service of the Great Republic, reserving to the States respectively, the Appointment of the Officers, and the Authority of training the Militia according to the discipline prescribed by Congress;

To exercise exclusive Legislation in all Cases whatsoever, over all Places purchased by the Consent of the Legislature of the State in which the Same shall be, for the Erection of Forts, Magazines, Arsenals, dock-Yards, and other needful Buildings;

To make all Laws which shall be necessary and proper for carrying into Execution the foregoing Powers, and all other Powers vested by this Constitution in the Government of the Great Republic, or in any Department or Officer thereof;

To Grant Reprieves and Pardons for Offenses against the Great Republic with the consent of three-fourths of each House; AND

To Audit Federal Agencies.

SECTION 8

The Migration of such Persons as any of the States now existing shall think proper to admit, shall not be prohibited by the Congress.

The privilege of the Writ of Habeas Corpus shall not, under any circumstances, be suspended.

No Bill of Attainder or ex post facto Law shall be passed.

No Imposts, Taxes, or Duties shall be laid on Articles exported to or imported from any State.

No Preference shall be given by any Regulation of Commerce or Revenue to the Ports of one State over those of another; nor shall Vessels bound to, or from, one State, be obliged to enter, clear, or pay Duties in another.

No Money shall be drawn from the Treasury, but in Consequence of Appropriations made by Law; and a regular Statement and Account of the Receipts and Expenditures of all public Money shall be published monthly.

Congress shall not create budgets for future years; Baseline Budgeting shall be strictly prohibited.

No Title of Nobility shall be granted by the Great Republic; No title of Office shall be retained by any Person after they have stepped down from said Office.

No Person holding any Office of Profit or Trust under them, whether at the National, State or Local level, shall accept any present, Emolument, Office, or Title, of any kind.

Congress shall make no law respecting an establishment of religion, or prohibiting the free exercise thereof; or abridging the freedom of thought, or of speech, or of the press, or of association; or the right of the people peaceably to assemble, and to petition the Government for a redress of grievances. The philosophy of political correctness, being contrary to the freedom of speech, shall not be permitted. Acts such as slavery, murder, theft, deception, and fraud, shall not be permitted under the guise of Free Exercise of Religion.

Congress shall make no law that makes a distinction in the burdens imposed or benefits conferred on any citizens by reason of birth, wealth, religion, sexual orientation, or political affiliation.

Congress shall not purchase or operate any corporation, either directly or indirectly, but shall encourage laissez faire free market capitalism.

Congress may interfere with corporations in only these ways: To ensure the products they produce are safe in their intended use, even though they may be unsafe in their unintended use; To ensure the products they produce actually do what they are supposed to do; To ensure the production of their products do not harm the environment; To prevent monopolies and price fixing; and To prevent crony capitalism. Congress shall have no authority to tell individuals or corporations what to produce, how much to sell their product, how much of the product to produce, or even to produce the product at all. The Legal Fiction of Corporate Personhood shall not be permitted.

Congress shall have no power to establish a Minimum or Maximum Wage.

Neither Congress nor any Government Agency shall give or donate any money, property, or material such as Subsidies and Foreign Aid to any individual, corporation, or organization, foreign or domestic, including foreign governments and State governments. Such voluntary donations by individuals, private organizations and corporations shall not be abridged, abolished or prohibited, subject to Article Four, Section Three.

Neither Congress, the States, nor Local Governments shall have the power to tax income. Neither Congress, the States, nor Local Governments shall make, or recognize, religious anti-defamation laws.

Congress shall make no law that gives advantage only to their members or where there is a conflict of interest with their members or for their personal gain. Congress shall make no law that applies to the citizens of the Great Republic that does not apply equally to the members of Congress, and Congress shall make no law that applies to the members of Congress that does not apply equally to the citizens of the Great Republic.

Congress shall make no law that forces or coerces one or more parties into contracts against their will.

Congress shall make no law, or accept any Treaty, that violates the Sovereignty of the Great Republic or the rights of the States and the rights of the people of the Great Republic.

Amendments and other changes to an Accepted Treaty shall require the Treaty be ratified again by Congress; Such changes shall not automatically become Law.

SECTION 9

Members of Congress shall be prohibited from junkets and other trips paid for by lobbyists, and are prohibited from receiving gifts, including meals, goods, and services, from lobbyists. All junkets and trips shall be approved, and paid for, by the Legislature of the State whom they were elected to serve.

SECTION 10

The Armed Forces of the Great Republic and the Militia shall be prohibited from executing laws, from becoming a national police force or civil guard, engaging in police actions, or otherwise performing the duties of civilian police in the Great Republic.

SECTION 11

Each Act of Congress shall contain a concise and definite statement of the constitutional authority relied upon for the enactment of each portion of that Act. The failure to comply with this section shall give rise to a point of order in either House of Congress. The availability of this point of order does not affect any other available relief.

SECTION 12

An Enumeration of the citizens shall be made in every year evenly divisible by ten. The sole purpose of such Enumeration shall be for Representation in each State. No personal, private, or other information, including but not limited to race, gender, and economic status, shall be demanded of the population; only Citizenship shall be questioned and only Citizens shall be counted.

ARTICLE 3

SECTION 1

The judicial Power of the Great Republic shall be vested in one supreme Court, and in such inferior Courts as the Congress may from time to time ordain and establish.

The Judges, both of the supreme and inferior Courts, shall hold their Offices for a term of ten years, and shall, at stated Times, receive for their Services, a Compensation, which shall neither be increased nor diminished during their Continuance in Office.

The Supreme Court and all inferior courts shall be composed of thirteen Judges. Every two years, the Supreme Court shall vote among themselves for the position of Chief Justice. No Judge may serve more than two years as Chief Justice.

SECTION 2

For each Vacancy on the Supreme Court, every State shall nominate a single Candidate within one week of said vacancy. Candidates from the States shall gather together and vote among themselves, with each Candidate having one vote, and no Candidate may vote for himself or herself. The Candidate with the most votes shall fill the vacancy immediately. In the event of a tie, a second round of voting shall take place with only those Candidates on the ballots.

No person shall be a Supreme Court Justice who shall not have attained the Age of forty-five Years, and been twelve Years a Citizen of the Great Republic, or a Citizen of the Great Republic at the time of the Adoption of this Constitution.

SECTION 3

The judicial Power shall extend to all Cases, in Law and Equity, arising under this Constitution, the Laws of the Great Republic, and Treaties made, or which shall be made, under their Authority; to all Cases affecting Ambassadors, other public Ministers and Consuls; to all Cases of admiralty and maritime Jurisdiction; to Controversies to which the Great Republic shall be a Party; to Controversies between two or more States; between a State and Citizens of another State; between Citizens of different States; between Citizens of the same State claiming Lands under Grants of different States, and between a State, or the Citizens thereof, and foreign States, Citizens or Subjects.

In all Cases affecting Ambassadors, other public Ministers and Consuls, and those in which a State shall be Party, the Supreme Court shall have original Jurisdiction. In all the other Cases before mentioned, the Supreme Court shall have appellate Jurisdiction, both as to Law and Fact, with such Exceptions, and under such Regulations as the Congress shall make.

The Trial of all Crimes, except in Cases of Impeachment, shall be by Jury; and such Trial shall be held in the State where the said Crimes shall have been committed; but when not committed within any State, the Trial shall be at such Place or Places as the Congress may by Law have directed.

SECTION 4

Treason against the Great Republic shall consist only in levying War against the Great Republic, or in adhering to their Enemies, giving them Aid and Comfort. No Person shall be convicted of Treason unless on the Testimony of two Witnesses to the same overt Act, or on Confession in open Court.

The Congress shall have power to declare the Punishment of Treason, but no Attainder of Treason shall work Corruption of Blood, or Forfeiture except during the Life of the Person attainted.

SECTION 5

The Judicial power of the Great Republic shall not be construed to extend to any suit in law or equity, commenced or prosecuted against one of the States of the Great Republic by Citizens of another State, or by Citizens or Subjects of any Foreign State.

SECTION 6

Supreme Courts, both National and State, shall neither suggest legislation, nor require legislation be passed. Supreme Courts, both National and State, shall not be told what Laws they can or cannot review.

SECTION 7

This Constitution shall be the supreme Law of the Land; the Laws of the Great Republic which shall be made in Pursuance thereof and all Treaties made, or which shall be made, under the Authority of the Great Republic shall be subject to this Constitution; and the Judges in every State shall be bound thereby, any Thing in the Constitution or Laws of any State to the Contrary notwithstanding.

Laws and customs of other nations and peoples, including religious laws, shall not be used when weighing Constitutional matters.

SECTION 8

In all cases decided by the Supreme Court and the inferior Courts, it shall be necessary for a minimum of seven members of the Court to concur.

SECTION 9

For the sake of expediency, the Supreme Court may take cases not yet decided by inferior courts.

ARTICLE 4

SECTION 1

No candidate who had been convicted of a felony shall be eligible for Elected Office, or candidate for the Supreme Court or any Inferior Court, or candidate for any Cabinet position.

No elected official, Representative, Senator, Vice President, President, Judge or Justice, who has been impeached and removed from office, shall be eligible to be elected or appointed to any public office.

No person shall be a Senator or Representative in Congress, or hold any office, civil or military, under the Great Republic, or under any State, who, having previously taken an oath, as a member of Congress, or as an officer of the Great Republic, or as a member of any State legislature, or as an executive or judicial officer of any State, to support the Constitution of the Great Republic, shall have engaged in insurrection or rebellion against the same, or given aid or comfort to the enemies thereof.

The Right of Citizens to Enforce the Qualification of any Candidate for the House of Representatives, Senate, Supreme Court Judicial Seat, President, or Vice President shall not be abridged.

The Senators and Representatives, and the Members of the several State Legislatures, and all executive and judicial Officers, both of the Great Republic and of the several States, shall be bound by Oath or Affirmation, to support this Constitution; but no religious test shall ever be required as a Qualification to any Office or public Trust under the Great Republic.

SECTION 2

Each State shall be responsible for the salaries of their Congressional Representatives and Senators and their staff. No State shall dictate, manipulate or force their Representatives and Senators, or their staff, by withholding or threatening to withhold said salaries if they do not vote a particular way on a Bill.

Congress shall be responsible for the salaries of the President and Vice President, including their staff, as well as the members of the Supreme Court and their staff. Said salaries shall come from the General Fund.

Under no circumstances shall the President, Vice President, Member of Congress, Member of the Supreme Court, their respective staff or any other public employee receive a pension or retirement plan from the National or State Government.

SECTION 3

No candidate for any Elected Office, at the National, State, or Local level, may receive campaign contributions or donations from any government, corporation, union, or other group source; No candidate may raise funds or campaign outside the territory of the Great Republic. No candidate, at the National, State or Local level, may raise or receive funds or campaign outside the Region they seek to represent.

Candidates may only receive campaign contributions from individual Citizens of the Great Republic. The maximum amount of Campaign Contributions a Candidate may receive from any individual Citizen shall be Five Thousand Republic Dollars. Candidates themselves shall be held to the same limitations on contributions to their own campaigns.

Campaign donations and contributions may be in any Form, from cash, services, banquets, and so forth, but are still limited to said maximum monetary value. These monetary values shall be adjusted every two years for inflation/ deflation. Citizens may donate to more than one Candidate.

Campaigns shall be run by the Candidates themselves. Private Citizens, Corporations, Unions, and Organizations shall not be permitted to publish articles or advertisements promoting or attacking a Candidate, unless the Candidate uses his or her Campaign Funds to purchase their services at Fair Market Value. Political Action Committees are prohibited.

Unions, corporations, organizations, including radio and television channels and newspapers, magazines, websites, et al, shall not be allowed to endorse any candidate as none of them have the right to vote.

Straw donations shall be prohibited.

Political Parties may not receive campaign contributions.

Donations to ineligible Candidates and all Campaign Funds not spent and Contributions and Donations in violation of this Section shall be deposited into the General Fund of the National Treasury if they were to be used in a National Campaign, or the General Fund of the State Treasury if they were to be used in a State or Local Campaign. Campaign Funds shall not be spent on anything unrelated to the campaign itself. A Candidate's unspent Campaign Funds may not be carried over to the next election cycle.

The source of all campaign donations must be listed publicly. No one shall be harassed, intimidated, or persecuted for valid donations.

Valid donations shall be considered Political Speech.

SECTION 4

Elections for President and Vice-President shall be held on the first Tuesday after the first Monday in November in every year evenly divisible by four, and elections for members of Congress shall be held on the first Tuesday after the first Monday in November in every year evenly divisible by two. The day of elections shall be a National Holiday.

Citizens must appear in person at their County Courthouse to Register to Vote. Upon Verification of Voter Eligibility the State shall provide, at no cost, a Voter Identification Card with the Citizen's Photograph on it. Counties shall not accept any Voter Registration within one month of any election. Citizens shall not be required to Register to Vote.

The Voter Identification Card shall have the Citizen's Photograph, Name, Address, Gender, and Year of Birth, in addition to a unique Identification Number, Dates the Card is Valid, and Congressional, City/Municipal, School, and Water Districts. The Voter Identification Card shall not be used for any purpose other than Voting in Primaries and Elections.

Early Voting shall be prohibited. Provisional Ballots and Absentee Ballots shall likewise be prohibited.

The right of Citizens of the Great Republic, who are twenty-five years of age or older, to vote shall not be denied or abridged by the Great Republic or by any State for any reason except for those who fail to Register to Vote and for those duly convicted of crimes and are currently imprisoned.

The right of Citizens of the Great Republic to vote in any Primary or other election for President or Vice President, or for Senator or Representative in Congress, shall not be denied or abridged by the Great Republic or any State by any reason other than failing to Register to Vote or being duly incarcerated.

All Primaries shall be held on the first Tuesday after the first Monday in June in every year evenly divisible by two. The day of primaries shall be a National Holiday.

Citizens must show their State-issued Voter Identification Card at their designated Polling Place in order to vote. Upon voting, whether in a Primary or General Election, the election clerk shall apply indelible blue ink to the left thumb of the voter, or other appendage approved by Law if it is missing. No Citizen may vote more than once in a Primary or General Election.

Aliens, as defined in Article Six, Section One, are ineligible to vote in any election.

The person in charge of elections, at the National, State and Local level, is to remain impartial and shall not let their own political affiliation influence their duty to ensure a fair election. Federal officials and employees may not use their official authority or influence for the purpose of interfering with or affecting the results of an election.

SECTION 5

No Candidate may run for more than one Office at the same time. No Candidate may run for one Office while holding a different Office, unless the term for that Office ends when the term for the other Office begins.

SECTION 6

Under no circumstances shall any Political Party have preferential treatment over another.

SECTION 7

All candidates for President, Vice President, House of Representatives, Senate, and Supreme Court, must have reasonable and sufficient understanding of the Constitution of the Great Republic prior to running for their desired position.

SECTION 8

The terms of the President and Vice President shall end at noon on the 20th day of January, and the terms of Senators and Representatives at noon on the 2nd day of January; and the terms of their successors shall then begin.

The terms for Supreme Court Justices shall end at noon on the 2nd day of January and the terms of their successors shall then begin.

SECTION 9

Gerrymandering shall not be permitted. Districts in each State must be even in terms of the Number of Citizens only and not based on political, religious, ethnic or other affiliations. No District may be more than fifteen percent longer or shorter than its width.

ARTICLE 5

SECTION 1

No State shall enter into any Treaty, Alliance, or Confederation; grant Letters of Marque and Reprisal; coin Money; emit Bills of Credit; pass any Bill of Attainder, ex post facto Law, or Law impairing the Obligation of Contracts, or grant any Title of Nobility.

No State shall lay any Imposts, Taxes, or Duties on Imports or Exports.

No State shall borrow money on credit.

No State shall, without the Consent of Congress, lay any duty of Tonnage, keep Troops, or Ships of War in time of Peace, enter into any Agreement or Compact with another State, or with a foreign Power, or engage in War, unless actually invaded, or in such imminent Danger as will not admit of delay.

SECTION 2

New States may be admitted by the Congress into this Union; but no new States shall be formed or erected within the Jurisdiction of any other State, nor shall any State be formed by the Junction of two or more States, or parts of States. A new State shall be admitted by a vote of two-thirds of both Houses of Congress and a vote of seven-tenths of the Citizens of the Proposed New State. The minimum population size of a region to be considered as a new State shall be no less than Six Hundred Thousand Persons and the minimum area shall be no less than One Thousand Square Miles. Congress may make exceptions to the Minimum Requirements only on a case by case basis.

Citizens of the Proposed New State that shall be admitted as a State in the Great Republic shall have the option of being granted Natural Born Citizenship while revoking their original Citizenship, or retain their original Citizenship and be considered Aliens within the Great Republic. Non-citizens of the Proposed New State shall retain their status as Aliens.

The Congress shall have Power to dispose of and make all needful Rules and Regulations respecting the Territory or other Property belonging to the Great Republic; and nothing in this Constitution shall be so construed as to Prejudice any Claims of the Great Republic, or of any particular State.

Any State that wishes to Secede from the Great Republic may do so only with the consent of three-fifths of the Citizens of said State. Congress may not prevent a State from leaving the Great Republic once the issue of Secession has passed with the consent of the Citizens of said State. Citizens in a State that Seceded shall have 30 days to retain or revoke their Citizenship status with the Great Republic.

SECTION 3

The Great Republic shall guarantee to every State in this Union a Republican Form of Government, and shall protect each of them against Invasion; and on Application of the Legislature, or of the Executive (when the Legislature cannot be convened) against domestic Violence. A Republican Form of Government being ". . . a government which derives all its powers, directly or indirectly, from the great body of the people and is administered by persons holding their offices during pleasure, for a limited period."

SECTION 4

Each State shall be responsible for the education of its people, but the people shall have the right to choose which school their children shall attend, or to home-school their children. Education shall not be run from or by the National Government.

Standards for Education shall include Physical Education, Reading, Writing, Math, Science, History, Geography, and Citizenship and shall promote Patriotism; schools may not prohibit the free exercise of religion; individual States shall be responsible for the standards of each grade level's requirements.

SECTION 5

The Citizens in each State shall have the right to recall their Representatives.

The People shall have no more than two months to gather signatures of twenty percent of the citizens in the district of the person they wish to recall. The Representative must be notified of the reason for recall before the people begin gathering signatures, in order to give that person a chance to respond to the charges. After the signatures have been collected, they must be verified independently, the verification process taking no more than one week to complete.

If the people have collected the required number of signatures, then a special election is to take place one week later, but only in the district of the person to be recalled. It shall be a "yes" or "no" vote whether to recall the person.. If the vote to recall passes by a simple majority, then that person has been recalled from Office and must step down immediately. At that time, the Legislature of their State shall fill such vacancy until the next election. The Legislature shall not fill the vacancy with the same person that was recalled.

A Representative shall be subject to recall only once per term. Being subject to recall shall mean it has gone all the way to an actual vote in that person's district.

Senators, being chosen by the Legislature of their State, are also subject to being recalled, but only by their State Legislature. The Senator being recalled shall appear before the State Legislature in order to respond to the charges. If the recall vote in the Legislature passes by a simple majority, then that Senator has been recalled and must step down immediately and the Legislature shall fill the vacancy until the next election. Senators shall not be limited in the number of times they are subject to recall.

SECTION 6

The States shall have the power to Repeal any Act of Congress. To Repeal an Act of Congress, a Bill of Repeal must be passed by three-fifths vote in each House of the State Legislature, by three-fifths of the States of the Great Republic.

SECTION 7

The States shall have the power to Reverse a Supreme Court Decision. To Reverse such

Decision, a Bill of Reversal must be passed by three-fifths vote in each House of the State Legislature, by three-fifths of the States of the Great Republic.

ARTICLE 6

SECTION 1

A Natural Born Citizen is a person born within the Territory of the Great Republic AND whose parents were BOTH Citizens AND each had resided in the Great Republic for a minimum of ten years at the time of his or her birth. The Territory of the Great Republic shall include Embassies and Consulates and Military Bases overseas, as well as ships and aircraft belonging to the Great Republic.

A Citizen is a person where one of his or her birth parents is a Citizen and said parent had resided in the Great Republic for a minimum of ten years at the time of his or her birth.

A Naturalized Citizen is a person who was not born a Citizen but was granted Citizenship by the Great Republic.

All Citizens in the Territory of the Great Republic at the time of the Adoption of this Constitution shall have the option of being granted Natural Born Citizenship while revoking their original Citizenship, or retain their original Citizenship and be considered Aliens within the Great

Republic. Non-citizens shall retain their status as Aliens.

Citizenship shall not be automatically given to those born within the Territory of the Great Republic. All Citizens of the Great Republic are Citizens of the State wherein they reside.

Citizenship shall not be obtained through adoption. If the adopted child could not be a citizen or Natural Born citizen at birth, their adoption shall not alter that fact, but they may become a Naturalized Citizen.

An Alien is a person residing in the Great Republic and is currently not a Citizen of the Great Republic. No Alien shall be allowed to hold any public office, either by appointment or election, from the Office of the President down to the local level.

The Great Republic does not recognize Dual Citizenship. Under no circumstances shall a Citizen of the Great Republic be a Citizen of another nation at the same time, as it presents a conflict of interest.

Under no circumstances shall a person who entered the Great Republic illegally be granted Citizenship by Naturalization. Illegal immigrants shall be deported and the country of origin shall be billed for the cost of their apprehension, detention, and deportation.

The Great Republic may not revoke a person's Citizenship, but a Citizen may voluntarily revoke their own Citizenship. The revocation of a Citizenship obtained through coercion or fraud shall not be recognized.

SECTION 2

The Citizens of each State shall be entitled to all Privileges and Immunities of Citizens in the several States.

A Person charged in any State with Treason, Felony, or other Crime, who shall flee from Justice, and be found in another State, shall on demand of the Executive Authority of the State from which he fled, be delivered up, to be removed to the State having Jurisdiction of the Crime.

SECTION 3

An armed and educated population being the bane of Tyranny, the right of the people to keep and bear Arms, including any and all types of ammunition and accessories, shall not be infringed except for those who, having been duly convicted, are currently imprisoned.

Arms shall include all types of hand-held firearms, whether single shot, semi-automatic, or automatic, and all types of non-firearm hand-held weapons, and defensive chemical weapons such as tear gas and pepper spray. Arms shall not include weapons such as cannons, missiles, rockets, mortars, artillery, flame-throwers, bombs and explosives, and chemical and biological weapons.

SECTION 4

No Soldier shall, in time of peace or war be quartered in any privately-owned house, building, or property, without the consent of the Owner.

SECTION 5

The right of the people to be secure in their persons, houses, papers, property, and effects, whether physical or electronic, including internet usage, against unreasonable searches and seizures, against spying and tracking, as well as data-mining and meta-data collecting, and against civil forfeitures, shall not be violated, and no Warrants shall be issued, but upon probable cause, supported by Oath or Affirmation, and particularly describing the place to be searched, and the persons or things to be seized.

No Citizen or Alien shall be required by the Government, Corporation, Union, Organization, or Individual, to allow them to spy on or track them as a condition for using their services.

No Citizen or Alien shall be subject to Internment or forced or coerced vaccinations. Nor shall any Citizen or Alien be required to undergo any medical procedure, excluding medical testing, against their wishes. Whosoever shall require a Citizen or Alien to undergo medical testing against their wishes shall do so only by the Due Process of Law and with respect to the other Provision of this Section and shall also be responsible for paying for said testing. The People do not belong to the Government.

SECTION 6

No person shall be held to answer for a capital, or otherwise infamous crime, unless on a presentment or indictment of a Grand Jury, except in cases arising in the Armed Forces or in the Militia when in actual service in time of War or public danger; nor shall be compelled in any criminal case to be a witness against himself, nor be deprived of life, liberty, or property, without due process of law; nor shall private property be taken for public use, without just compensation. Public use shall not include economic development or other methods to increase tax revenues. Private property taken for public use shall not be turned over to another individual, company, union, or organization.

SECTION 7

No person shall be subject for the same Offense to be twice put in jeopardy of life or limb; nor shall any person be tried in both Civil Court and Criminal Court for the same Offense.

In all criminal prosecutions, the accused shall be informed of his or her rights when arrested, and enjoy the right to a speedy and public trial, by an impartial jury of the State and District wherein the crime shall have been committed, which District shall have been previously ascertained by law, and to be informed of the nature and cause of the accusation; to be confronted with the witnesses against him; to have compulsory process for obtaining witnesses in his favor, and to have the Assistance of Counsel for his defense. In all cases, the accused shall be considered innocent until proven guilty.

SECTION 8

In Suits at common law, where the value in controversy shall exceed fifty Republic Dollars, the right of trial by jury shall be preserved, and no fact tried by a jury, shall be otherwise re-examined in any Court of the Great Republic, than according to the rules of the common law. This monetary value shall be adjusted for inflation/deflation.

SECTION 9

Excessive bail shall not be required, nor excessive fines imposed, nor cruel and unusual punishments inflicted. Capital punishment shall not be permitted.

SECTION 10

Neither slavery nor involuntary servitude shall exist within the Great Republic, or any place subject to the jurisdiction of the Great Republic, including involuntary servitude in "public works, " or the Armed Forces. Whether in times of Peace or War, service in the Armed Forces shall be entirely voluntary. Slaves and involuntary servants entering the Great Republic shall immediately receive their freedom.

The sole exception to the prohibition against involuntary servitude is service in the Militia.

No Citizen or Alien, either living, in the womb, or deceased, in whole or in part, shall be considered Property of any Government, Corporation, Union, Organization, or any other Person.

SECTION 11

No Citizen or Alien shall be required to join any corporation, union, or organization for any reason.

Workers must be protected without regard to whether they are unionized. The right to work is the right to live. A person may not be denied employment based on membership or non-membership in a labor union. The right of a person to work may not be denied or abridged because of membership or non-membership in a labor union or other labor organization. In the exercise of the right to work, each person shall be free from threats, force, intimidation, or coercion. A person's inherent right to work and to bargain freely with the person's employer, individually or collectively, for terms of the person's employment may not be denied or infringed by law or by any organization.

A contract that permits or requires the retention of part of an employee's compensation to pay dues or assessments on the employee's part to a labor union is void unless the employee delivers to the employer the employee's written consent to the retention of those sums. A contract is void if it requires that, to work for an employer, employees or applicants for employment: (1) must be or may not be members of a labor union; or (2) must remain or may not remain members of a labor union.

A labor union, a labor organizer, or an officer, member, agent, or representative of a labor union may not collect, receive, or demand, directly or indirectly, a fee as a work permit or as a condition for the privilege to work from a person who is not a member of the union.

"Labor organization" means any organization in which employees participate and that exists in whole or in part to deal with one or more employers concerning grievances, labor disputes, wages, benefits, hours of employment, or working conditions.

Under no circumstances shall public employees, meaning those who are employed by the government, whether National, State or Local, be permitted to form or join labor unions or similar organizations.

Efforts to Unionize employees must be done through Secret Ballot, to prevent employees from harassment, coercion, intimidation, and retaliation by Union Organizers and Employers.

SECTION 12

Citizens and aliens alike shall be free from torture, both physical and mental. Torture being defined as "any act by which severe pain or suffering, whether physical or mental, is intentionally inflicted on a person for such purposes as obtaining from him, or a third person, information or a confession, punishing him for an act he or a third person has committed or is suspected of having committed, or intimidating or coercing him or a third person, or for any reason based on discrimination of any kind, when such pain or suffering is inflicted by or at the instigation of or with the consent or acquiescence of a public official or other person acting in an official capacity. It does not include pain or suffering arising only from, inherent in, or incidental to, lawful sanctions." (Convention against Torture and Other Cruel, Inhuman or Degrading Treatment or Punishment, United Nations, 10 December 1984)

Spanking, as a form of corporeal punishment to cause temporary pain on a child's buttocks, and used by a parent or guardian to discipline their child, does not constitute Torture or abuse.

SECTION 13

No Citizen or Alien, Government, Corporation, Union, or Organization shall be exempt from paying taxes owed to the Great Republic.

ARTICLE 7

SECTION 1

Full Faith and Credit shall be given in each State to the public Acts, Records, and judicial Proceedings of every other State. And the Congress may by general Laws prescribe the Manner in which such Acts, Records and Proceedings shall be proved, and the Effect thereof.

SECTION 2

No State shall make or enforce any law which shall abridge the privileges or immunities of citizens of the Great Republic; nor shall Congress, any State, or any individual deprive any person, born or in the womb, of life, liberty, or property, without due process of law; nor deny to any person within its jurisdiction the equal protection of the law.

SECTION 3

The validity of the public debt of the Great Republic, authorized by law, shall not be questioned. But neither the Great Republic nor any State shall assume or pay any debt or obligation incurred in aid of insurrection or rebellion against the Great Republic; but all such debts, obligations and claims shall be held illegal and void.

SECTION 4

The powers not delegated to the Great Republic by the Constitution, nor prohibited by it to the States, are reserved to the States respectively, or to the people. The Great Republic does not have any powers not specified by the Constitution. The enumeration in the Constitution, of certain rights, shall not be construed to deny or disparage others retained by the people.

SECTION 5

Socialism, Communism, State-ism, and any other form of state collectivism, being the antithesis to Free Market Capitalism, are specifically outlawed. Political parties based on these principles shall have no legal standing and shall not be recognized as legitimate.

SECTION 6

Secret Police, Secret Courts or Tribunals, and Secret Prisons shall be prohibited.

SECTION 7

For the sole purpose of uniformity, English shall be the Official Language of the Great Republic;

this shall not mean that English is the Only Language used in the Great Republic.

SECTION 8

The rights of one citizen or a group of citizens shall not be abridged "for the greater good." This Constitution shall not be set aside for any reason. No National, State or Local Government, or agency thereof, shall declare Martial Law. Military officers and enlisted personnel shall not have authority over civilians.

SECTION 9

Except in times of War, any Territory held by the Great Republic that is not a State shall have no more than one year from the time it became a Territory in order to become a State, otherwise it shall be released as its own Nation.

SECTION 10

International Laws and Treaties with foreign nations shall not violate, infringe, overlap, or usurp the Sovereignty of the Great Republic, the rights of the individual States, the rights of the People, and this Constitution. All such laws and treaties shall be held null and void and unenforceable. The People of the Great Republic and the Great Republic itself shall not be subject to foreign Governments, including International Governments. Members of the Militia and Armed Forces of the Great Republic shall not serve under foreign commanders or serve in foreign units.

ARTICLE 8

As granted by Article 5, Section 3 of this Constitution, "The Great Republic shall guarantee to every State in this Union a Republican Form of Government." Each State Constitution shall be laid out in similar fashion to this Constitution. The State Constitution shall be required to have the following items in order to be considered for Statehood by the Congress of the Great Republic:

To promote, but not require or demand, Patriotism, the Constitution, and Good Citizenship.

Rights specifically granted or denied in the Constitution of the Great Republic shall be applied to the States and People of the Great Republic.

All elected officials, from the Governor down to the City Council Members, plus all judges, shall have term limits. The members of the State Legislature shall have the same term limits as the Congress. The State Supreme Court Justices shall have the same term limits as the National Supreme Court Justices. The Governor and Lieutenant Governor shall have the same term limits as the President and Vice President.

All Bills in the State Legislature must conform to the same rules as in Article Two, Section Six of the Constitution of the Great Republic.

Cities shall not be allowed to annex property without the consent of three-fourths of those living in the area to be annexed.

ARTICLE 9

The Congress, whenever two-thirds of both Houses of Congress shall deem it necessary, or on the Application of the Legislatures of two-thirds of the several States in the same year, or by popular vote of two-thirds of the several States in the same year, shall Propose Amendments to this Constitution, which, in either Case, shall be valid to all Intents and Purposes, as part of this Constitution, when ratified by two-thirds of the vote by the Legislatures in two-thirds of the several States. If the proposed Amendment is not passed, then it must wait no less than five years before being proposed again.

The Process for Amending the Constitution shall not be Amended.

ARTICLE 10

The Ratification of the Convention of at least two States shall be sufficient for the Establishment of this Constitution.

CHAPTER 3

WHAT WAS I THINKING!?

In this chapter, I will be discussing many of the things I determined needed to be changed in the Constitution of the United States. They will be presented according to the articles in the Constitution of the Great Republic, found in chapter two. Please note that only those Sections or Subsections that have been changed will be discussed.

THE PREAMBLE

To start with, I changed the Preamble completely. I felt it was needed because some people had started using the phrase, "to promote the general welfare," as an excuse to justify their premise that the government "must provide welfare" to the people. There is no real justification for this notion. Nowhere in the rest of the United States Constitution does it give Congress or the President power to provide welfare to anyone.

The Preamble does not actually grant powers. All it does is give a statement of why the framers wrote their Constitution. So, in that spirit, I chose to take a piece of the Declaration of Independence and use it in the new Constitution.

"We hold these truths to be self-evident, that all people are created equal, that they are endowed by their Creator with certain unalienable Rights, that among these are Life, Liberty and the pursuit of Happiness, and that the Government of the Great Republic derives its just powers from the consent of the governed."

The reason I chose that piece is that it shows where our Rights come from and where the Government derives its Powers. If our rights come from people, then the people in power can take them away. Since our Rights come from our Creator, no President, no Legislature, and no Court, can take them away from us!

ARTICLE 1 - THE EXECUTIVE BRANCH

First and foremost, in Section 1 of Article 1, I drastically altered the Electoral College. The current Electoral College System is based on representation in Congress, with the number of Representatives plus the two Senators, so if a state had eight Representatives and two Senators, that state would have ten Electoral Votes. Whichever candidate won the election in that state would ordinarily receive all ten Electoral Votes. However, they are 'votes' and sometimes those appointed to the Electoral College do not vote in accordance with the way their state voted.

Unfortunately, some states have started looking at altering how their Electoral Votes are given, so that it will no longer be an "all or nothing" distribution. They want to change it so that if one candidate received

55% of the vote and the other candidate received 40%, the Electoral Votes would be distributed in the same percentages.

What these states are proposing is changing the Constitution of the United States in a manner not prescribed by the Constitution of the United States!

Now, in the new Constitution, the state in the above example would have eight Congressional districts, one for each Representative, and whoever won in each District would receive one point in the general election. I felt it would put the elections closer to the People and it does not give anyone the option to change the results by voting differently in the Electoral College.

This change would take the voting for president out of the hands of the states entirely. It also means that candidates won't be able to target a few specific states, such as California, Texas, New York, Pennsylvania, and Florida, in order to win the general election. I am also hoping it would make cheating and vote fraud more difficult.

In Section 2, I changed an important aspect of the Presidency. I removed the power to Pardon. How can one man Pardon someone who had been convicted by a jury of his peers? It enables one person to be able to override such convictions and opens the door to corruption, especially if the person to be Pardoned is a friend or is politically connected. The purpose of re-writing the Constitution was to shut as many of these doors as possible. Power corrupts and I want to limit how many in our government become corrupted.

The other change was to allow the House of Representatives a say on Treaties. I decided to deal with Treaties the same way as legislation, requiring both Houses to pass it with the consent of three-fifths of their members. Please note that Treaties must be approved by both Houses of Congress and the President does not have the power to override the decision by Congress. Anything less than a Treaty, such as the Agreement with Iran that Barack Obama made in his second term in office, shall not be enforceable. The President may not "legislate" by Agreements.

The text from Sections 3 and 4 were unchanged from the original Constitution.

Section 5 was created to answer a problem. Nothing was ever said in the United States Constitution on what happens if the President or Vice President were ever found to be ineligible for office. I give the authors of that constitution a lot of credit for what they achieved, but they could not think of everything.

I have linked both the President and Vice President together, as they both campaigned and were elected on one ticket. They would be immediately replaced by the ticket that came in second place. Anything they signed, or vetoed and not over-ridden by Congress, would be presented to the new president and vice president. An over-ridden Bill automatically becomes Law, regardless of who the president is.

The text from Sections 6 and 7 were unchanged from the original Constitution.

In Section 8, I have given the President the Line Item Veto power on any appropriations bills, the bills that spend money. They have wanted it, and needed it, for a long time, but Congress kept rejecting it in order to keep the pork flowing. The items vetoed can be overridden in the same manner as an entire Bill that has been vetoed.

Section 9 deals with Executive Orders. I feel there has to be some restraint on this Power. According to the Federal Register of the National Archives, Barack Obama, during his first four years as president, has issued 144 executive orders. George W. Bush issued 291 in eight years, Bill Clinton issued 364 in eight years, George H. W. Bush issued 166 in four years, and Ronald Reagan issued 381.

These orders have the potential to violate the Separation of Powers. I understand that some of them are very necessary for the president to conduct business, especially urgent business, but they should not be above review. So I put limits on them. They shall not be used to spend money or prevent the spending of money, nor can they modify a Law, as those Powers resides with Congress. And the President cannot alter how a Law is enforced in order to circumvent it. Finally, I have given Power to the Supreme Court to review them directly.

In Section 10, I made a change to the Executive Departments. Right now, the "Executive Departments" are composed of fifteen cabinet positions and six others with cabinet-rank. The current fifteen departments are: State, Treasury, Defense, Justice, Interior, Agriculture, Commerce, Labor, Health and Human Services, Housing and Urban Development, Transportation,

Energy, Education, Veterans Affairs, and Homeland Security.

The six cabinet-rank positions are: Chief of Staff, Environmental Protection Agency, Office of Management and Budget, Trade Representative, the US Ambassador, and the Council of Economic Advisors. This last group, the Council of Economic Advisors, sounds like a bunch of sycophants and czars.

And speaking of czars, I found out that they date back to Franklin Roosevelt's administration, but only recently have they gotten out of hand. George W. Bush, by one account had about thirty-three, while Barack Obama had nearly forty! How many of them were approved by the Senate? Why were they considered necessary when there were entire Departments available to deal with their issues? And who pays for them?

In my opinion, there are only four Executive Departments that are truly necessary and these four listed here are the same ones created by George Washington. They are: Justice, State, Treasury, and War. Yes, I mean War. It is the War Department. Why? Because making War is the role of the military, whether it is on offense or defense. To keep the name "Defense Department" is to suggest the role of the military is only to defend the country. That much is true, but they also say that the best defense is a good offense. I guess someone decided to change the name to keep it from sounding too "aggressive" to others. War is aggression and if attacked, I hope the Great Republic would respond aggressively.

Secondly, I would now require all appointments to these four posts to be approved by three-fifths consent by both Houses of Congress. And lastly, I am preventing all Agencies and Departments from issuing rules that have the same effect as a Law, as that is the duty of Congress.

The last thing I added to Article 1 is Section 11, the *War Powers Act*. The fighting going on in Iraq and Afghanistan is (or was) happening without a formal declaration of war, just like the actions in Korea and Vietnam. At this time, the United States is not officially at war with anyone. I have acknowledged the fact that at times the President has to use military force for the safety and security of our people and our assets overseas. The President has done so in the past, such as in Grenada and Panama, and most of the time they have been extremely limited in scope.

The Korean Conflict, Vietnam Conflict, the two Iraq "wars," and the "war" in Afghanistan have corrupted the meaning of War and the United States Constitution. For sustained military action, the government must vote for a Declaration of War. Do it right or don't do it at all!

Let's be clear about one thing: if we had declared war in Iraq and Afghanistan, then those people captured in combat would be Prisoners of War, not languishing in Guantanamo Bay, Cuba, in a faux, and quite possibly illegal, prison. Naturally, the enemy, being caught not in uniform, could be shot as spies, if we were in a declared war. But we aren't (or weren't) so they remained "terrorists" and subject to . . . what?

ARTICLE 2 - THE LEGISLATIVE BRANCH

Now we're on to Congress. The famous quote from the movie, *Star Wars*, "you will never find a more wretched hive of scum and villainy" can be applied to this branch of government. Of course they would take offense to it. Then again, how many people go into Congress poor and retire millionaires? How many use their offices to make money for themselves, family members, and friends? Insider trading anyone? Or pass legislation that benefits them, directly or indirectly, or their friends and family?

Is this libel? Absolutely not! For one thing, it is not said maliciously, nor directed at anyone or any political party in particular. Second, if none of them did these things, then why do they have a panel on ETHICS? I don't mean to imply that ALL members of Congress are crooks, but then again, look at their approval ratings. How many have been there for more than ten, twenty, thirty years? Power corrupts and the "Good Old Boy" system is alive and well in the United States Congress.

In the Constitution of the United States, Article 1 outlined the Legislative Branch and was the largest article in the entire document. I moved it to Article 2 and it is still the largest article in the document. That is because most of the power in both governments resides in the Legislative Branch.

The changes to the Legislative Branch begin in Section 2. In the United States Constitution, Article I, Section 2 states that the number of Representatives shall not exceed one for every thirty thousand but each State shall have at least one Representative.

With a population of over three hundred million, we should have at least ten thousand Representatives! Why don't we have that number? Because of a Statute, a Law?

If that is the case, then that Law is unconstitutional! Only an Amendment can change the Constitution and there has been no amendment to allow this.

The only other explanation is that they interpreted 'shall not exceed' to mean there can be less than one per thirty thousand. I wanted to specify an exact number for the House of Representatives, but then realized that the Senate would continue to grow with the population while the House would remain fixed, so I threw that idea out.

With a population of three hundred million people, one per six hundred thousand would give a house membership of five hundred, a more or less reasonable number. Yes, it's an arbitrary number, but so is one for every thirty thousand!

Section 2 also discusses vacancies in the membership of the House of Representatives, so I wanted to clarify the matter on who is responsible for filling it. I wanted to leave the process to the individual state legislatures, rather than having a new election, or having one individual, a governor, appointing the replacement.

I threw in Term Limits in Section 2, because I felt that political service is just that: service! The original writers, I believe, never intended there to be career politicians. I included a limit on service in Leadership in the House, after I heard something like that on Sean Hannity's radio broadcast. The actual leadership position does not matter. No politician can serve two years as Majority Whip and then two years as Speaker of the House, but they can serve for one year in each.

And as for Impeachment, the Senate tries the case and the House determines punishment, so I thought I would clarify that a bit, too, while I was at it.

And now for the Senate. In Section 3, I increased the number of Senators by fifty percent. Why? Why not? Their six year terms are split anyway so why not create a third Senator and have their elections every two years?

As for electing Senators, I wanted to restore the original intent of the United States Constitution, which was amended by the Seventeenth Amendment in 1913. The House of Representatives was to be the voice of the People, while the Senate was meant to be the voice of the States. This is a Federal System, not a straight democracy! With the change in 1913, the States pretty much lost their voice in the Federal System, which is NOT what the framers intended. The Constitution is a system of Checks and Balances, to prevent too much power from being wielded by any one person or group.

I also clarified the procedure for filling vacancies and clarified the procedure for Impeachments, plus more Term Limits! Included was the same restriction on serving in leadership positions.

The text from Section 4 was changed to prevent both Houses of Congress from changing their rules in the middle of their session and to eliminate the voice vote and a vote by show of hands.

Section 5 states that members of Congress, in all cases except treason, felony and breach of the peace, are prevented from being arrested during their attendance at the session of their respective houses and going to and returning from them. This was to prevent the manipulation of a vote, and other such abuses, but that does not exempt them from paying fines and fees. Too many members of the United States Congress have outstanding fines and fees, including parking violations and bank overdraft charges, and they use their office, their position, to avoid paying them. How many members of Congress haven't paid back their student loans? And what about their staffs? Are they exempt from paying theirs, too? That's just not right. This change should bring such things to an end.

Here, in Section 6, is one of the biggest changes in the Constitution. In Congress, I have severely limited them on what they can do regarding Bills, specifying how many votes they need to pass a Bill, how many they need to repeal a Bill, and the process of merging the Bills from both houses. In order to quickly weed out bad Bills, I made it easier to repeal a Bill than to pass it. No president may block the repeal of a Law.

As for the process to merge Bills from both houses, it stemmed from the process Congress used to pass the Affordable Care Act. Normally, each house would pass its own Bill and then send them to a Conference Committee which unified them, and then the now identical Bills would be sent back to both houses to be ratified. With the Affordable Care Act, the House of Representatives, with a vote by a simple majority, merely accepted the Senate version, instead of risking another vote on the issue. They sidestepped the Conference Committee altogether, using bureaucratic methods because they saw nothing wrong with it and because they knew they didn't have the votes to pass it the right way. It was expedient. That should not be able to happen in the Great Republic.

I also wanted to clarify something else a bit more, as I found the language in the United States Constitution's Article I, Section 7, to be a bit confusing.

If any Bill shall not be returned by the President within ten Days (Sundays excepted) after it shall have been presented to him, the Same shall be a Law, in like Manner as if he had signed it, unless the Congress by their Adjournment prevent its Return, in which Case it shall not be a Law.

This makes it sound as though if the President does not sign a Bill within ten Days after it is presented to him, it shall automatically become a Law. I didn't like that idea, so I increased the time to twenty-one days and then declared that if the Bill was still not signed, it would automatically be Vetoed.

Next, I limited the size of every Bill in Congress to fifty standard letter size pages, single spaced with a twelve point font and with a specific line height and spacing and margins. I was so specific because I know how those in Congress like to find ways around obstacles, if not outright ignoring them. I believe that if they think they can get away with something, they will eventually try.

I also prohibited Riders, Amendments and Attachments to Bills so that the Bill covers only one subject. For example, if a Bill requesting that a bridge be built across a specific point over a specific river in Alaska, it cannot contain provisions for railroad crossings in Alabama or other bridges in Alaska. This should also prevent the Bill from referencing other documents, to bypass the size limitation (as in "see Document X, pages Y through Z, for further details").

The size limit on the Bills was imposed because I was tired of Congress creating Bills and including all sorts of unrelated items. Sometimes they may add a pet project to a Bill they knew others felt had to be passed, such as a bill funding the soldiers fighting in Iraq and Afghanistan. Then there was the one thousand-page Stimulus Bill in early 2009 (the so-called the Porkulus Bill). But it wasn't the last thousand-plus page Bill to hit Congress.

There was no way anyone could read what was in these huge Bills in the time allotted. Reading it non-stop for a week, perhaps, but with the legal mumbo-jumbo that they love to put in (in spite of the fact that the legal profession is currently moving away from "legalese") there would be no way anyone could do it and still understand what was in it. As for the length itself, that was easy. The Constitution of the Great Republic, with those same standards, is only about thirty pages long.

I also felt that if something needed to be passed, if it was good, it could stand on its own. Most aren't and they put in Riders and Amendments to make it more palatable to others. That is wrong. I am not stopping pork with this Constitution, but it will have the effect of making it more obvious. They will be less likely to sneak things through in Bills that are easy to read.

Then I required that every bill be available to the public for reading seventy-two hours in advance, giving the members of Congress, and their constituents, time to read it, unlike the political theater of the "2012 Fiscal Cliff" deal that was given to Congress just three MINUTES before they voted on it! I don't think any of the members of Congress read it before they voted on it. And who was it that campaigned on the promise to give three days' notice to the public before Congress voted on the bills? How long did he take to break that promise? Answer: Barack Obama and about one week (if not sooner) into his first term in office!

No Bill should be rushed through Congress. Please note that a Declaration of War is not a Bill. Naturally, the corrupt politicians would not like this provision, as they would no longer be able to hide their actions or avoid accountability to their constituents.

Section 7, describing the "Enumerated Powers," was also heavily modified. It's counterpart, Article 1, Section 8 of the United States Constitution, says that Congress has the power to lay and collect taxes. It does not specify what it can and cannot tax. As is currently the case, they have taxed nearly everything under the sun. Since they collect so much in taxes, they are finding creative ways to spend it while at the same time trying to find new things to tax. Even money we put into Social Security (whether we want to or not) gets taxed when it is doled back out.

The first change I made was in limiting Congress' Power to Tax. By limiting the items that can be taxed and the amount they can tax it, it will help eliminate waste and corruption. Besides, taxing all goods sold by corporations or organizations is the most fair. Everyone will be paying it, including those who are here illegally! And one more thing, I had to put a definition of "goods" into the Constitution because that word itself was rather vague and vagueness runs counter to the entire concept of this project - clarity.

Goods are physical, tangible items other than money or real estate. Yes, under this definition food would be considered a "good", as would gasoline and heating oil, but attorney fees would not. I didn't want the government to come in and say, "That dollar bill is a physical and tangible object that was created, therefore we can tax it."

I also didn't want Congress to establish permits, fees, licenses, and other such terms, as a means of taxation, and I limited the Tax Rate to ten percent. Why should the government receive more than we tithe to God?

As for taxing property, a friend of mine once said that we should be taxing property because in the grand scheme of things, the country owns the property outright, as a matter of "Sovereignty", even though individuals and corporations have titles to individual pieces. But I believe that if the government taxes us annually on property we "own", then we do not really own the property but are actually "renting" it from the government, which runs counter to our way of life.

Besides, if the government actually owns the property, then doesn't that give them the right to dictate everything done on and to that property, including how we live our lives? My house, my rules? That concept would destroy the United States and it would destroy the Great Republic, too.

Now, keep in mind that the Gross Domestic Product for the United States in 2014 is said to be about $17.4 trillion dollars. If Consumer Spending accounts for two-thirds of it, that means that the people spend about $12 trillion each year on goods and services. The remaining third is comprised of government and corporate spending.

With a maximum taxation rate of ten percent, the government of the Great Republic would take in over a trillion dollars each year in taxes. Some would say that is too little, but with a lot of the overhead eliminated, it should be enough to cover everything else that is the responsibility of the Government. The ten percent rule is the maximum rate. Congress has the power to set it lower if they want. But I wouldn't hold my breath.

On the question of Government borrowing money, the answer is no. The government cannot borrow money, unless it is for a war effort. Congress must first declare war, and the money borrowed must be used to prosecute the war. They cannot be allowed to declare war and then shuffle the budget around so that they can spend money on other things while they are at it.

To prohibit Congress from borrowing money from foreign creditors keeps foreign interests out of the country's business. They can't say, "Well, you owe us, so we get a say in how you run your country, otherwise we'll call your debt and collapse your economy!" This will force Congress to BALANCE THE BUDGET!

During War, I would rather not be hindered by a balanced budget, especially if it means the difference between winning and losing!

Next, Congress originally had the power only to establish a uniform rule of naturalization. The constitution said nothing about immigration. According to the Tenth Amendment, that Power should have been reserved to the States, but the Federal Government has broken that one, too. Just look at what the Government did when Arizona tried to enforce the immigration laws. Arizona was shut down, as it was the "role of the federal government," or so the argument went. The Federal Government wasn't enforcing the laws and Arizona tried to do what the Feds did not and got busted for it. So I made a change to my constitution so that Congress could officially have the Power to be able to determine who can legally enter the Great Republic. In my mind, it is a matter of national sovereignty that would give Congress that right. I also didn't want to have fifty different rules of immigration, either.

There have been many people who have said that many of our problems started when we left the Gold Standard. There was nothing on which to really base the value of the currency. Its value was what we said it was. Also, the United States Congress has delegated its authority over Money to the Federal Reserve, which is unaccountable to everyone, including Congress! The Federal Reserve, somehow, is preventing Congress from auditing their books! The Congress of the Great Republic could not do such a thing.

In addition, I decided to identify the new currency as the Republic Dollar. Its symbol could be a stylized "R".

In another subsection, dealing with the military, I described the Armed Forces of the Great Republic, the Republic Marines. What I see today is unnecessary duplication in staffing and equipment between the Army, Navy, Air Force, Marines, and Coast Guard. You have different uniforms, different ranks, and different chains of command. I wanted to unify everything under one tent, making everything more standardized and streamlined.

I decided to include the definition of "Militia" in the Constitution since nobody really wants to recognize it in the United States Constitution, especially in the context of the Second Amendment! Whereas the Republic Marines are strictly volunteer, the Militia may be "called out", or drafted. But the draft in regards to the Militia is limited to suppressing insurrections and repelling invasions. As a result, the Militia may not be used outside the borders of the Great Republic. This constitution does not give the Government the power to roll the Militia into the Republic Marines, either.

Among one of the powers of Congress is the phrase, "To make all Laws which shall be necessary and proper..." Please read that carefully. It says "necessary AND proper." Some Laws may be necessary but are not proper, and some are proper but not necessary. It must qualify on both counts.

As for the Power of Pardon, I have never agreed to these last minute pardons the Presidents of the United

States give out as they prepare to leave the White House when their terms end. Some of those pardoned really did not deserve to be pardoned and received it through back room deals or one-sided arguments. By giving this power to Congress and requiring a specific and high percentage to pass, it is my hope that it prevents those who don't deserve it from receiving pardons while allowing those who may deserve it to receive it, while reducing the possibility for corrupting officials in the process.

And lastly, I have given the power to audit all federal agencies to Congress. Hopefully, this should have the effect of curbing the abuse of power by any and all agencies in the federal government.

In the new Section 8, my so-called "Section of No's," one change I really wanted to make to the United States Constitution was the stipulation that under no circumstances shall the Writ of Habeas Corpus be suspended. Not many people realize that during the Civil War, Abraham Lincoln suspended the Writ of Habeas Corpus. I find it quite strange that no one successfully challenged him on that. If anyone had, I sure haven't heard of it. Nowhere does the Constitution of the United States give the president, or Congress for that matter, the power to suspend any part of the Constitution itself!

I have incorporated the First Amendment directly into the constitution, but with a twist. I abolished the concept of "political correctness." I also covered acts that might be used under the guise of "freedom of religion."

There are those who love to "abuse the system" or try to twist it to their advantage.

Please note that freedom of religion includes the freedom to choose your own religion, to change religions, and to have no religious beliefs. It does not include freedom FROM religion, in the context of keeping religion out of the "public eye." Those who are pushing THAT idea are "anti-religious," not atheists, which is odd because it is their belief that there is no God, and their beliefs are better than everyone else's.

Next, our economic system is supposed to be free market capitalism. Naturally, the Socialists and Communists abhor it, even though it is proven to work whereas theirs has proven to fail. Repeatedly. They try to confuse the people by equating free market capitalism with crony capitalism, which is where companies and politicians conspire together to create legislation favorable to their business at the expense of other companies and individuals. I want to keep the government out of the way of business. Let a business fail or succeed on its own. There is no such thing as "Too Big to Fail!" If a business is failing, it is for a reason and propping it up does not solve the problem!

I did see to it there are five controls over corporations to keep them from running amok, because I know that some people are greedy and don't care who gets hurt on their way to making a buck. One control is regarding product safety, that it is safe in its intended use; second is regarding advertising, that the product does what it is supposed to do; third to limit pollution; fourth is to prevent monopolies and price fixing; and fifth is to prevent crony capitalism.

Then there is my idea regarding corporations; there will no longer be such a thing as "corporate personhood." Corporations are not people and don't have human rights. Will this prevent a person from suing a corporation? Probably, but they could then sue the corporation's chief executive officer, the board of directors and other members of the corporation. Those people would not be protected from lawsuits.

And lastly, there is the minimum wage. Congress, according to the United States Constitution, has NO authority to set the minimum wage. Commerce Clause? No. That regulates interstate commerce. It does not give the government the authority to tell companies how much they should pay their employees. Such power shall not exist with this Constitution either.

The next subsection prohibits government from giving foreign aid, subsidies, bailouts and the like to companies, organizations, foreign governments, and individuals. This does not prevent Congress from paying the salaries of the president and vice president and other government employees and officials, including military personnel.

Neither governments, corporations, organizations, or individuals shall be dependent upon the government of the Great Republic for financial or material support. It doesn't stop individuals, in their individual capacities, from such donations, but they would be doing so with their own money, not the taxpayer's money.

I know, this would be one that the corrupt would love to "misinterpret" to their advantage or someone else's disadvantage. Our government should not be in the business of "propping up" other governments. Sometimes, the proceeds do not actually go where they are supposed to go, ending up instead in the pockets of the dictators and their cronies that rule those countries. Or worse, end up in the hands of terrorists who want to kill us because some members of the foreign government are their allies.

This subsection shall also be used to eliminate Social Security, Medicaid, Medicare, and ALL other "social" programs, including welfare. This will probably be the most controversial and condemned part of this new Constitution. The bleeding heart liberals will shout at the top of their lungs, "how dare you!" But the role of government has never been to take care of its citizens in this fashion! It was, and still is, a matter of personal responsibility and family responsibility! Yes, people can fall on hard times and need help, but that is where families and the church (charities) step in!

If you will bear with me, I am not really dissolving such programs. I am just removing the funding, and the control over them, from the government, from the taxpayers. I, personally, would like to see charities set up to take over these programs and let people donate as much, or as little, as they want into them!

No one will be required to donate to these charities. Only in a tyrannical and totalitarian system does the government make its people dependents! Besides, how much fraud goes on in these government-mandated systems? How many people who are able to work, don't work in order to receive Welfare? How many women have a lot of children in order to receive more benefits? How many people here in this country illegally are receiving government benefits?

The next subsection explicitly abolishes the income tax. It essentially repeals the Sixteenth Amendment, which was passed February 2, 1913. Income is basically trading time from your life in exchange for monetary gain. So taxing income is essentially taxing someone's life, making them subjects and not citizens.

The following subsection takes away a source of bullying by religious extremists that I see being used in other countries. I don't want to see it here, as it conflicts with freedom of speech. Please keep in mind that by doing away with religious anti-defamation laws, it does not mean people can lie about other religions. Libel and slander laws still apply.

The next subsection, is as follows:

Congress shall make no law that gives advantage only to their members or where there is a conflict of interest with their members or for their personal gain. Congress shall make no law that applies to the citizens of the Great Republic that does not apply equally to the members of Congress, and Congress shall make no law that applies to the members of Congress that does not apply equally to the citizens of the Great Republic.

This subsection prevents Congress from passing laws that applies to the people but not themselves, or laws that apply to them and not the people. There are two examples that come to mind right now. One is Social Security. Everybody pays into it, except Congress (plus teachers and perhaps other public or government employees). The other is health insurance. They tell us what kind of insurance we can have, but it doesn't compare with their own. Members of Congress shall not be exempt from their own legislation!

I have to admit that the first sentence in that subsection was mine. The rest was in an e-mail that was floating around and I could not resist including it. I do not know the source, but it was concise.

Next, I prohibited Congress from passing any law that would force or coerce one or more parties into contracts against their will. This was my attack on the Affordable Care Act, which tells me what kind of insurance I MUST have. I haven't heard of anyone speak about being forced into a contract, but purchasing health insurance is just that - a contract between yourself and an insurance company.

In the last part of Section 8, I am upholding the Constitution of the Great Republic above any and all treaties. No treaty should be above the Constitution, nor have the power to take away the rights of the states or the rights of the people. And any time a treaty, which has been ratified by the Great Republic is amended, the entire treaty and its amendment must be ratified again in order for the changes to take effect.

Members of Congress love to go on trips. Whether these trips are paid for by lobbyists or the taxpayer, it does not seem to matter. I wanted to put a limit on these junkets, and did so in Section 9.

In my opinion, if the junket is a valid trip, their home state shall approve it and pay for it. If not, they cannot go. I also wanted to curtail the "bribery" of officials by the lobbyists. This paragraph makes a good attempt at prohibiting lobbyists from unduly influencing Congress. The alternative would be to ban lobbyists altogether.

In Section 10, I dealt with the use of the military to enforce laws. The military, traditionally, has been trained to fight, kill, and destroy. It was never meant to be a police force. The armed forces and the Militia are for conducting warfare, not keeping the peace and "nation-building". They are not trained for it. And no, they cannot be "deputized" and serve under law enforcement officials, as that is also outside their chain of command.

Section 11 is the Enumerated Powers Act (HR 450) that John Shadegg of Arizona proposed. It has been brought up multiple times and Congress has left it to die in committee each time.

Lastly is Section 12. Under the Constitution of the United States, the government can ask, or demand in some cases, just about anything they want on the census and historically the information is hardly private, even though they say it is. I believe the census is currently being used as a data mining tool.

My proposed correction would limit the census takers on what they can ask everybody: "Are you a citizen of the Great Republic?" If the answer is yes, they are counted. If not, they are not counted. It is as simple as that. The sole purpose of the census is to count the citizens for the purpose of determining representation. Aliens, whether legal or not, shall not be counted.

ARTICLE 3 - THE JUDICIAL BRANCH

I have made some major changes to the Judicial Branch of government. First, in Section 1, instead of a lifetime appointment for judges, they will now have a term of ten years. No one should be able to serve a lifetime in government.

As for the number of justices on the Supreme Court, someone noted that the United States Constitution does NOT specify the number of members of the Supreme Court. They were quite correct, so I came up with a specific number: 13.

When asked, "Why thirteen judges on the Supreme Court?" I responded with several answers. First, it was good enough for Jesus and the Apostles; second, it is a prime number; third, the number thirteen is a lucky number (for me); fourth, my father was born on the thirteenth; fifth, it will (hopefully) get people away from triskaidekaphobia (fear of the number thirteen) and lastly, it is more than nine and should lend more brainpower to resolving issues.

In Section 2, I changed how vacancies on the Supreme Court are filled. Under the United States Constitution, the president (actually, the people serving the president) selects a candidate and that candidate is grilled by Congress before being accepted or rejected. The Supreme Court is supposed to be the third branch of Government. Why do they have to be subject to appointment and approval by the other two branches?

Neither of the other two branches has to submit to this kind of procedure. So I did the following:

> *For each Vacancy on the Supreme Court, every State shall nominate a single Candidate within one week of said vacancy. Candidates from the States shall gather together and vote among themselves, with each Candidate having one vote and no Candidate may vote for himself or herself. The Candidate with the most votes shall fill the vacancy immediately. In the event of a tie, a second round of voting shall take place with only those Candidates on the ballots.*

This change will take the issue out of the hands of the politicians in the capital and bring it down to the state level. Each state shall determine how their candidate is nominated. This may give rise to corruption at the state level but ought to require a lot more of them to be corrupt in order to affect the whole process. We are relying on the honesty and good judgment of the state governments to appoint qualified and honest judicial candidates. The method of each candidate having one vote and they cannot vote for themselves should help weed out the bad judges.

The text from Sections 3, 4, and 5 were unchanged from the original Constitution.

According to Section 6, courts will be unable to demand, or even suggest, laws be passed, and they shall not be told what laws they cannot review. This is the core of the Separation of Powers. The Judicial Branch cannot legislate, and the Legislative Branch cannot prevent courts from ruling on their laws.

This came about because of what happened a few years ago. I heard that the Supreme Court of Massachusetts told their State Legislature they must enact a specific Law. I believe it had something to do with the issue of gay marriage. Regardless of the issue itself, the Court was wrong in telling the Legislature what to do. Equally wrong is the Legislature telling the Courts what laws they can and cannot review.

In Section 7, I have upheld the Constitution as the supreme law of the land. All laws and treaties passed by Congress shall be subject to the Constitution. Under no circumstances are they to supersede the Constitution.

Some say that a few of our Supreme Court justices actually cite foreign court decisions when settling matters in the United States, as if our Constitution must be interpreted from the position of other nations or the UN. If a crime was committed in the Great Republic, by people from other nations, the laws of those nations should not apply, as a matter of sovereignty. This section should put a stop to that practice.

Right now, under the United States Constitution, it only takes a simple majority, five out of nine, to concur. In Section 8, I have continued with that tradition, but with the increased number, it will be seven out of thirteen that will need to concur.

In Section 9, I have given the Supreme Court a power that I don't believe they currently have, or if they do have it, they don't use it very often. I have given them the power to weigh certain matters even if those cases haven't gone through a lower court yet. I felt it would be better to let the Supreme Court deal with issues immediately rather than have to wait for a court battle, and then go through the lengthy appeals process, before they could take the case. For one thing, there are many cases I would love to see resolved right now, such as reviewing the origination challenge to the Affordable Care Act, but they are taking years to go through the process.

ARTICLE 4 - THE ELECTORAL SYSTEM

As you might have guessed, this is an entirely new article and deals with the subject of elections. I felt it had to have its own article because of all the ways the current system has been corrupted.

In Section 1, I describe who is not qualified for office. Those who have been convicted of a felony, or impeached and removed from office, shall not be eligible for any elected office or cabinet post. It should have the effect of kicking criminals out of government and keeping them out. A pardon does not undo a conviction.

Next, I have allowed citizens to bring suit to resolve the qualifications of these officials. There are some who argue that Barack Obama was not qualified to serve as president, due to the Natural Born Citizen clause, and the courts have repeatedly quashed the concerns by saying these people lack "standing." I may not be understanding the term "standing," but I feel that "We the People" should have the right to enforce the Constitution, even when our elected officials refuse to do so!

Perhaps the courts were unwilling to open up the argument that they DO have the power to remove the president if he fails to be qualified. Some in the courts are thinking that only Congress can remove the president and only through impeachment. I believe the courts can remove a president if he or she has attained the office even though they are not qualified to hold it.

In Section 2, I changed how members of Congress and their staff get paid. I got tired of Congress trying (and frequently succeeding) to give itself a raise when the people were not looking, so I made their home state responsible. This means that a senator from Rhode Island may get paid less than a senator from California, but then their cost of living is also different. For one thing, a house in Texas that costs $100,000 may run more than $1 million in New York.

Also, knowing how manipulative people can get, I wanted to prevent their home state from dictating to their members in Congress how they should vote. They cannot hold their salary over them. That is blackmail and is also against the law.

As there are term limits for everyone in government, I have specifically prohibited them from receiving pensions or retirement plans from the national or state government. They cannot receive taxpayer money after they have left office.

Section 3 is all about Campaign Finance Reform. It was initially because of Hillary Clinton. In the 2000 election, Hillary Clinton campaigned for the New York Senate seat in some strange places. I know for a fact that she came to McAllen, Texas, to do some campaigning.

The local press interviewed some of the people who attended her event and one comment struck me as outrageous. Someone said that when she is elected to the Senate, she would look out for "our" interests. My reaction was, "What?! She is going to look out for the interests of New York, not Texas!" She also campaigned in California and elsewhere and raised a lot of money doing it. Why was it necessary for her to do that? Couldn't she raise any money in New York? I am sure she's not the only one who has done this. She's just the only one I've actually seen do it.

But Hillary Clinton was not the only reason for creating Section 3. Another reason has to do with who is donating to our politicians. It is my contention that corporations, unions, and organizations are not individual people. They do not have the right to vote in an election, the citizens do. So why do they have the right to participate in elections?

Let's take the abortion issue. Within a union, how many members are pro-choice and how many are pro-life? Not everyone in the union will have the same beliefs. What if that union chose one of these positions and gave money to a candidate that supported it? What say do those in the union who are opposed to that position have? Is it right for the union to use your dues to support a cause you are opposed to? It is the same with corporations. Most of the time, the board of directors and the shareholders have different, sometimes opposing causes and beliefs. Is it right for the company to support one and oppose the other?

Some may call this "censorship" but who am I really censoring? Name the "person" I am censoring! The one you name may be the CEO of the company or the union boss, but they are not the corporation or the union. They are individuals.

As for campaigns, they have gotten so expensive these days it seems you need to be a millionaire (or billionaire) in order to afford to run for any office. I wanted to limit donations to ALL candidates! The wealthy candidates will be restricted in the use of their own money on their campaigns as well, in order to keep a level playing field. If I didn't restrict the use of personal funds, then we will once again be at a point where only the wealthy could run for office!

I am not limiting how many people can donate, but I am restricting donations to citizens. Non-citizens, also known as citizens of foreign nations, do not have the right to vote, so they should not get to donate to any candidate. It doesn't matter how long they have lived here.

Candidates shall no longer be able to enrich themselves with campaign funds. I remember a particular senator from Illinois who began the race for the White House. When he started, his personal wealth was estimated to be about four hundred thousand dollars. When the race was over, his personal wealth was several million. Gaining wealth is not the purpose of government; nor is running for office a way to gain wealth.

I am imposing a lot of limitations on elections, in the hope of dissuading the crooked and corrupt from seeking office, and from manipulating any election in their favor.

Lastly, I am requiring that all sources of campaign contributions be listed publicly. Barack Obama is the reason for this little paragraph. Under the current system in the United States, he received a lot of little donations, amounts of twenty-five dollars or less in the 2008 election cycle. He and his campaign staff never bothered to identify the source of these donations. Right or wrong, it was speculated that some may have come from overseas, from countries such as China, Iran, or Saudi Arabia, which is clearly illegal, but they were not required to screen them because of the size of the donation, never mind the quantity. If such a thing happened, it was because they "played" the rules.

In Section 4, I got into the voting process. Some will find my decisions to be "controversial" or "discriminatory," but deep down they really aren't. They are common sense answers to modern day corruption.

For instance, how many people do not get out to vote because they are working on election day? They don't want to get mixed up in the mad rush at five o'clock so they just go home. How many wait in line for hours after the polls were supposed to close simply because they could not vote until they got out of work? I have made it into a national holiday, so they can go vote whenever they want, up until the polls close. Hopefully, it would improve voter turnout.

Next, I changed how the people register to vote. They must appear in person at their county courthouse and the state shall provide a Voter Identification Card.

It's pretty much the same as getting a driver's license, complete with picture.

I am also stopping all voter registration within one month of the election day. There is a very good reason for this: ACORN. In the 2008 election cycle, this so-called "Association of Community Organizations for Reform Now" submitted hundreds or thousands of registration cards up to the last minute, gaining provisional ballots. They overwhelmed the people responsible for verification, which was the very purpose of dumping the cards on them at the last minute. I wanted to put a stop to it, especially after ACORN was accused of registering the entire front line of the Dallas Cowboys offense in the state of Nevada!

There will not be any registration within one month of the election, early voting, provisional and absentee voting will likewise be banned. As election day is a National Holiday, you will have no excuse for not being able to vote. I know there will be plenty of people "out of town" during election day, and some of it can't be helped, but the purpose here is to reduce fraud, and I think there has been plenty of it in the early, absentee, and provisional voting process. I'm sorry, but my response to that excuse is "too bad." Plan better next time. Say no to moves around election day. It is on you. Also, keep in mind there is no requirement to register to vote, and no requirement to vote. Only a dictatorship will force people to vote, even if there is only one candidate.

Then I changed the voting age to twenty-five. I can hear it now, "What are you thinking? I can't vote until I am twenty-five? Are you crazy?" Well, I've heard it said that age twenty-five is the age of reason. Think about it. Insurance rates are pretty high until you reach at least twenty-five, especially among men. Why? At age twenty-five, you are more settled down, you are out of school (for the most part), and you have more experience in the world.

It is the experience that separates twenty-five from eighteen. At eighteen, you are just out of high school. You may know a lot of facts, but many lack maturity and experience. At age twenty-five, you are less easily manipulated. I know that at age eighteen you think you know everything, but there's so much more to learn.

And one more thing, why was the voting age changed from twenty-one to eighteen? The 26th Amendment changed the voting age simply because the young people were told they were not old enough to vote or to drink alcohol, yet were being drafted to fight and die in Vietnam. In this Constitution, conscription is only allowed in regards to the Militia, in suppressing an insurrection or repelling an invasion. Service in the Republic Marines is strictly voluntary, plus there is no mention of any drinking age. That issue is something for the individual states to decide as it is not one of the Enumerated Powers.

Now, as with the election day, the day of the primaries should also be free from rushing around, so I also made it a national holiday. I put the primaries on a specific day, the first Tuesday after the first Monday in June, for a very good reason, and that is to prevent what happened in the 2008 election.

When the primaries began in the spring of 2008, there were about nine Republicans and ten Democrats (more or less) running for office. When Texas finally got around to its primaries, there were roughly three Republicans and two Democrats remaining. The one I wanted to vote for had dropped out long before they got to Texas and I felt deprived, disenfranchised.

Putting all the primaries on one day is like putting all your eggs in one basket. The candidates have one shot and one shot only and should make the best of it. They can have their convention immediately after the primaries in order to select their nominees for office.

I know some people will not like being required to show a photo ID in order to vote. Then again, they are the ones with the reputation of saying, "Vote early and vote often." Besides, everyone will receive an ID card when they register to vote.

What may really get these people upset is the use of indelible blue ink at the polling place. My thoughts on this are, well, if it is good enough for third-rate dictator countries like Iraq, then it is good enough for us. Besides, it will help ensure that a person does not vote more than once! The blue ink requirement will be applied in both the primary and general elections.

Under Section 5, no candidate may run for more than one office at a time. In the 2008 election, how many candidates for one office were holding onto another office at the same time? Barack Obama, Joe Biden, Sarah Palin, John McCain, and the list goes on.

Those who lost the election stayed in office and those who won left an empty seat behind to be filled by someone else instead of through a proper election. These politicians like to remain in office as long as possible and holding onto one seat while running for another is like having a lifeline. If their aspirations fail, they can keep going in the old job. It's a form of "job security." This is selfish in the extreme. They are doing it for themselves, not for the people they are supposed to be representing.

In Section 6, I have taken away the power of the big two political parties. Between the Democratic and Republican parties, they virtually control the elections. And now it seems there is very little difference between them. Those in Congress seem to vote the same, regardless of party. They just talk a big game.

And the media is no help, either. The media harps constantly that a vote for a third party candidate is a vote thrown away or wasted. Such rhetoric is a form of intimidation, to keep people voting only for candidates in the two "real" parties.

These two parties get preferential treatment by the media as well as the government in general. Sometimes I think it is a conflict of interest that the ones in power look after the interests of the party that "got them into office" rather than the people who actually got out and voted for them and really got them into office.

As it currently stands, for a third party to run on a ballot, they have to go through hoops such as coming up with a minimum number of people who support the candidate. They have to do this each election cycle. The two "real" parties are exempt. If a third party candidate misses the deadline for registering in a state, that candidate cannot get on the ballot, but for candidates in the "real" parties, they get waived on through. Barack Obama and John McCain BOTH missed the deadline for registering in Texas in 2008, but they got on the ballot anyway. They should have been held to the same standards, or even held to THE standards set forth by Texas. This is one form of preferential treatment that ends in the Great Republic!

In Section 7, I want people responsible for governing to have a reasonable understanding of their powers and limitations of their powers. Determining this can be as simple as having a candidate take a multiple-choice test. Each question on the test has four answers, one right and three wrong. I don't like the ones where there are two wrong answers and two right answers but one is more right than the other.

Once a candidate/office holder has done this, he or she won't have any excuses when they introduce legislation that exceeds their authority, rules against something obviously constitutional or issues executive orders that violate the constitution. It is a level of accountability to the voters. Will some candidates cheat? Probably, but they will still be on record as "knowing what they are doing."

In Section 9, I am specifically outlawing gerrymandering! I know, there already are laws on the books against it, but sometimes they are not being enforced! Just look at the 28th Congressional District in Texas in 2006! It stretched from McAllen, Texas northward all the way to San Antonio, but does not include San Antonio itself! How does this strangely drawn district represent the Rio Grande Valley region? It doesn't! It looks like it was artificially drawn - it's not natural! People have been manipulating the system for generations and only occasionally getting busted. Hopefully, this restriction on the size, both in population and geography, of the districts will do more for killing gerrymandering than what we currently have.

ARTICLE 5 - THE POWERS OF THE STATES

The text from Section 1 was unchanged from the original Constitution.

The US Constitution is rather vague on the entry of new states into the union. Section 2 changes that. I have dictated that the new state must have a minimum of 600,000 citizens, but there is no maximum population. The minimum size of the proposed new state is to prevent a lot of tiny states being added, but I have allowed Congress to waive that rule. I didn't want it to be used to exclude islands from becoming states.

The minimum number of votes needed by the prospective state is relatively high, at seventy percent, but I did it to ensure that most of the citizens there want to join and won't cause problems later. If the percentage was lower, say sixty percent, that would mean that around forty percent were not happy and that could spell trouble, perhaps in the form of violent insurrection.

The requirement for both houses of Congress to approve the new state is to ensure that a new state is welcomed with open arms instead of forcing themselves on the rest of the country.

The rest of Section 2 means that Iowa, for example, cannot split into East Iowa and West Iowa, or North and South Dakota merging into Dakota, or Missouri adding a piece of Kansas, without their legislatures' approval, but once their legislatures approve, then it would go to both houses of Congress and a vote of the people of the proposed new state or new state borders.

As they are free to join, they should be free to leave. In fact, it's a little easier to leave than enter and Congress has no say on whether they can or cannot leave. I would rather let a state leave in peace than force them to stay at gunpoint. That does little to endear them to you. Besides, if they cannot leave, then what does that make them? Property. Slaves. And both are unconstitutional. Therefore, states must have the right to leave.

Section 3 was in response to George W. Bush. He was always using the phrase, "spreading democracy." Sure, he wasn't the only one using it, but he used it a lot. I hope nobody in the future will get this mixed up. The country is not a democracy but a republic. There is a difference. I felt there had to be a definition of a republican form of government, to keep future generations from "redefining" it.

The Federalist #39 defines a Republican Form of Government as ". . . a government which derives all its powers, directly or indirectly, from the great body of the people and is administered by persons holding their offices during pleasure, for a limited period." A

Democratic Form of Government is defined as "...a form of government in which the supreme power is vested in the people and exercised directly by them or by their elected agents under a free electoral system." A Democratic Form of Government is more akin to Majority, or Mob, Rule.

I tackled education in the next section. I believe government cannot do many things right. In the United States, the federal government cannot run the school system properly. They throw more and more money at schools with no improvement in the results. It is insanity. Then they come up with things like, "No Child Left Behind." Now it has become politicized with "Common Core." Education should be left to those closest to the problem and that is NOT the national government.

For Section 5, I decided to do something to allow the people in each state to recall their senators and representatives. I tried to think of everything regarding the process to recall. No member of Congress should disregard the will of the people in their state. The people are the ones they are supposed to be representing!

In Section 6, I gave the states the power to repeal an act of Congress. As this is a Republic, a federal system of government, I felt that the states should have the power to override Congress, if necessary. So, when Congress refuses, or is unable due to gridlock, to repeal an act, then it shall be the right of the states to come in and override the will of Congress.

And lastly, Section 7 gives the states the power to overturn a Supreme Court decision. The Supreme

Court does make mistakes from time to time. Case in point: *Dred Scott*. I have made the process difficult, but not impossible, in the belief that if the Supreme Court made a bad decision, a lot of people would recognize it as such, and it most likely then would not be difficult to overturn it.

ARTICLE 6 - THE RIGHTS OF THE PEOPLE

These are specific rights granted to the people, but is not meant to be a definitive list of all their rights! As you may guess, these originated from the first ten amendments to the United States Constitution, commonly known as the Bill of Rights.

A good definition of citizenship was missing from the US Constitution and has created a headache for many constitutional scholars, so I included it as Section 1 of this Article. I put a ten-year residency requirement to prevent someone from being naturalized, then returning to his home country and conferring citizenship on his children, and they, in turn, never actually coming to the Great Republic, but conferring citizenship on their children. I believe that if you are going to be a citizen, you have to at least spend some time here.

The Law of Nations (Le Droit des Gens) by Emerich de Vattel, published in 1758, was the basis for the definition of "natural born citizen." Scholars know this to be fact, but some people wanted Barack Obama to become president, so they changed the definition to mean a citizen who has not gone through the naturalization process."

Now, since I clearly defined Natural Born Citizen, I felt I had to define Citizen, Naturalized Citizen, and Alien.

Some people will be upset with this section because it also puts an end to the so-called "anchor babies," which is a term given to children born in the United States to mothers who are not citizens. The mothers hope that being the parent of a US Citizen would prevent the government from deporting them .

I have also restricted aliens from serving in government. I felt that would be a conflict of interest, since their allegiance is with a foreign government, not the Great Republic.

I have banned dual citizenship for the same reason. Having a British-Great Republic citizenship, one would have split loyalties. It is a conflict of interest. Yes, I am forcing people to take responsibility and choose a side.

Lastly, I have put in writing that anyone who enters the Great Republic illegally shall never be allowed to become a citizen. For one thing, those who enter illegally have clearly shown a disregard for the laws of the country.

The text from Section 2 was unchanged from the original Constitution.

Section 3 has the next big change and will have many people upset, as it has to do with the right to bear arms. The Second Amendment to the US Constitution has been interpreted several different ways. I don't think the original writers intended it to be that vague, but there it is. I have elaborated on it and, hopefully, made it abundantly clear.

Tyrants hate an armed and educated citizenry. Most tyrants eliminated privately owned weapons before they made their move so that the people would be unable to stop them. Hitler, Stalin, and Mao all did this and look at what they did to their own people and to others around them. About a 100,000,000 people, unable to defend themselves, were killed by their own governments.

I feel that the people have a right to many of the same weapons as the national government, but I have made some exceptions. I don't think the people need cannons, artillery, explosives, bombs, missiles, rockets, and chemical and biological weapons.

I freely acknowledge that criminals will get a hold of these same weapons and use them to commit crimes, but they are doing that already. The only difference is that now the people will have equal firepower. Besides, the police cannot be everywhere at once. To really stop crime, you need to have an officer on every street corner, and there are a lot of street corners. As one person put it, there are more law-abiding citizens than there are criminals.

All the statistics I have ever seen point to the fact that when a city (or nation) bans personal firearms, crimes increase (check out Australia for example) and when they are mandated or simply allowed, crimes decrease. Criminals generally look for the easy targets. You know, the ones where the owners can't shoot them as they are breaking in! Gun Control: Creating a "safe work environment" for criminals. Criminals don't want to get shot any more than we do, and the nut cases want the freedom to commit their mass shootings unimpeded. That's why they don't attack a gun shooting range. Gun-Free Zones: Creating a "target-rich environment" for mass murderers. When seconds count, help is minutes away.

Some will argue that weapons must be banned to protect children from accidentally shooting each other, but my argument is that more children die from drowning in a five gallon bucket than from guns. More people die in automobile accidents each year than from guns. Should we then ban all cars and trucks from the road?

I do have a provision that allows criminals to own weapons, but only AFTER they have served their sentence. Why do people insist on punishing them after they are released? If they are that bad, then their sentences should have been longer. Prisoners may lose many of their rights and privileges while in jail, but why don't they get them back when they are duly released?

And before I leave this issue, let me ask a rhetorical question: "How can disarming law-abiding citizens stop criminals from committing crimes using weapons?" Criminals, by definition, will not obey the law and turn over their weapons! So the law only applies to...law-abiding citizens!

The text from Section 4 was unchanged from the original Constitution.

Section 5 covers the 4th Amendment to the United States Constitution, but I expanded it to cover advances in technology and modern abuses, such as electronic property, data mining and meta-data collecting.

Many things were done in the past that were just plain wrong, and the people knew it. One example was the internment of the Japanese on US soil during World War II by Franklin Roosevelt. That was not a power of the government, but I think that some in government believe that if it is not mentioned in the Constitution, they still have a right to do it, rather than the other way around.

I do not like the government forcing people to have a vaccine. Governor Rick Perry tried that once and, fortunately, the Texas legislature put a stop to it. Other governors were more successful. I felt the requirement was based on money, not science or health.

One company pushing their vaccine had just lost a multi-billion dollar lawsuit on their heart medicine, which the suit claimed had killed patients. Then they come out with this vaccine and start lobbying heavily to have the government mandate it. It looked to me like they were trying to recover the money they had lost, rather than helping people.

So I included that when I was modernizing the search and seizure amendment to the US Constitution. Many of these changes apply to the state and local levels as well. No doctor can perform a medical procedure without the consent of the patient, no matter who is standing next to him ordering him to do so. Medical testing is slightly different but no less invasive. Some tests include the breath test for drunk driving. That is a legitimate medical test. But even while allowing testing to take place, I am also preventing the victim (in the case of those unwilling to undergo the testing) from having to pay for these tests. If the government wants to have someone undergo a medical test, then the government (TAXPAYERS) must first get a warrant and the government has to pay for it. I wanted to make it perfectly clear to tyrants that the governed do not belong to the government.

Section 6 is based on the 5th Amendment to the United States Constitution. The change I made to it is found in the second part of this section, and was a direct result of *Kelo v. The City of New London*, where property owners were forced out in order for a private company to build a new shopping center, all because the city would take in more in taxes from a shopping mall than it did from the homeowners. This was not the intent of eminent domain and I wanted to make sure it never happens again.

Section 7 covers double jeopardy. I changed it slightly because of what I saw as an injustice in the case of O. J. Simpson. He was tried for murder in criminal court and then tried AGAIN, but in civil court. I believe they were splitting hairs in order to get around double jeopardy. The only difference was that if found guilty in criminal court, the defendant would go to jail, but in civil court, the punishment would be financial in nature. He was still tried for the same offense twice!

As I see it, the victim's family wanted revenge, especially when Simpson was released. Whether he was actually guilty or not is not the issue. Double jeopardy is the issue. They should have to choose either civil court or criminal court. Either way, the person still ends up in court. I also hate the term "wrongful death." I consider it word-spinning.

Section 8 has also been altered slightly. The Seventh Amendment to the US Constitution reads "twenty dollars." That was back in 1791. I thought it could be raised up a bit, at least to fifty Republic Dollars, and then have allowances made for inflation and deflation of currency.

The text from Section 9 was unchanged from the original Constitution.

Section 10 covers the 13th Amendment, but gives it a big boost. The governed do not belong to the government. This includes their parts, because I know how those in government think. They will try just about anything to get around restrictions. That's why we're in the mess we are in right now. This section abolishes that which the original US Constitution failed to do - slavery. It also prohibits the government from drafting people into the armed forces, but not the Militia. If the government wants to get the country involved in a conflict, it had better make sure it is for the right reasons, otherwise it may find itself without enough military strength to finish the job. This is intended to limit the number of conflicts in which the Great Republic gets involved. The Militia exemption is for the sole purpose of defending the Great Republic from invasion and insurrection.

Much of Section 11 comes from the right to work language I found the State of Texas using. I wholeheartedly agree that no one shall be forced to join a union, nor be denied the right to join one. I do not agree with Card Check, which eliminates the right to a secret ballot vote on whether to create a union or not. Card Check will enable both the union and the corporation to intimidate or harass an employee who did not vote the way they wanted him or her to vote.

My personal feelings are that unions have a valid place, confronting bad corporate practices, but some have also been corrupted by money and power, actively prevent bad employees from being fired, and drive up costs for the company. Right to Work is supposed to protect the employees, essentially, from both the bad corporations and the corrupt unions. I know the unions would be upset with me saying they are corrupt, but my reply would be in the form of one name: Jimmy Hoffa.

Section 12 covers the issue of torture. I'm usually opposed to anything coming out of the United Nations, but this one stuck with me - banning torture and defining what torture is. This section prevents the government from torturing ANYONE, not just citizens or people living in the Great Republic. Also, it doesn't matter WHERE the prisoner is being held. If they are held by personnel of the Great Republic in another country and those people are being tortured, those doing the torture can and should be arrested and tried in court. I also don't want to see the 'outsourcing' of torture, by turning over prisoners to a third party so they can be tortured. Banning torture is meant to protect prisoners and prisoners of war.

This does not outlaw parents spanking their children because spankings, in general, are not severe. I make a distinction between spanking a child and beating a child.

Section 13 prevents people, governments, corporations, and unions from being exempt from paying taxes. It may seem like a ridiculous thing to add, but I believe it is necessary. For instance, I hear about "manifestos," here on the border of the Rio Grande, and how they are used by Mexican nationals to recover the taxes they paid on goods they purchased in this country. I may be wrong about it, but this is the intent behind this section. Nobody should be above paying taxes, especially after the taxation power has been severely amended in this Constitution.

ARTICLE 7 - THE MISCELLANEOUS PROVISIONS

In this Article, you will find a lot of miscellaneous provisions I wanted to see in the new Constitution. Some are from the original Constitution of the United States.

The text from Sections 1 and 2 were unchanged from the original Constitution.

In Section 3, I removed the language referencing pensions and bounties, as government pensions are prohibited in a previous section.

The text from Section 4 was unchanged from the original Constitution.

In Section 5, I am outright banning socialism, communism, state-ism and other forms of state collectivism, and I have my reasons. For one thing, if people weren't so "human" then perhaps socialism and communism might work, but we are and they won't.

It is human nature to work harder for higher rewards. No rewards is worth no work. If you don't get paid, why bother working? That is the key flaw in socialism and communism. Once people find out they are working so someone else does not have to, then more people will stop working or slack off. It is a cascading effect until very few are working and more are unemployed and living off of them. The government will then have to force people to work or they will be killed. In a sense, those working so the others don't have to is a form of economic SLAVERY.

Also, these types of governments do not like competition, or criticism. How many people died under Hitler? Millions. Mao? Millions. Stalin? Millions. Pol Pot? The list goes on.

Human nature is the drive for socialism and communism (control) and it is the reason it fails (selfishness and greed). It will always fail, no matter how noble and "utopian" someone makes them sound. Many people will put in the least amount of work necessary to achieve their goals. The higher the goal, the more they will work to get it. The lower the goal... well, you get the picture.

Free Market Capitalism does not guarantee success, only the opportunity for success. Crony Capitalism manipulates the system to guarantee success for a select few at the expense of everyone else, so don't get the two confused.

In Section 6, I banned secret police, secret courts, and secret prisons. Anything that resembles the Gestapo and Star Chamber is specifically ruled out. For one thing, secret police generally are charged with spying on the citizenry, which is outlawed in Article Six, Section Five. The Star Chamber (secret tribunals) is banned under Article Six, Section Seven. I wanted to leave no doubt about these. And secret prisons? I mean the 'black sites' scattered in countries around the globe. I mean Guantanamo Bay prison for terrorists. I mean military prisons housing civilians. They are specifically abolished.

In Section 7, I made English the official language of the Great Republic, specifically, American English. This is not meant to prevent people from speaking other languages in this country. In fact, I would encourage the learning of other languages. All I mean with this is that in official documents and street signs, English shall be used. Many street signs use symbols, which is okay, but for those with writing on them, the language should be English. The purpose, as stated, is unity. People must be able to communicate with each other.

In Section 8, I have banned martial law and the setting aside of the Constitution, and ruled out the excuse that it is for the greater good. A lot of evil things have been done "for the greater good." Hitler exterminated Jews, gypsies, and the handicapped because he felt it was "for the greater good." During the Civil War, parts of the US Constitution were set aside "for the duration." No government shall declare martial law. The military is not allowed to exercise jurisdiction within the Great Republic. It is not for law enforcement and is strictly prohibited from that role. The military can still police its own bases, but not the streets of a city or the countryside. Nor can it give civilians orders. It's not their job.

In Section 9, I am banning the Great Republic from becoming an imperial power. Territory must become a full-fledged state or be cut loose. As it now stands, Puerto Rico, Guam, American Samoa and the American Virgin Islands, among others, are territories and have been for decades (to say the least). It is my belief that they should, as the saying goes, "fish or cut bait", join or leave. This provision will prevent these territories from being quasi-states, with many of the benefits as if they were states, but without the obligations of being states. I would tell them they can't have it both ways.

For Section 10, international laws and treaties shall not trump the Constitution of the Great Republic, or the rights of the people of the Great Republic. I am setting up the Great Republic to be above international laws and treaties with foreign governments. No other government would make itself subservient to foreign powers, and neither should we.

I also don't agree with the Republic Marines fighting under the UN banner. It's a conflict of interest and the UN is not accountable to anyone in the Great Republic. Right now, there are problems with US soldiers not wanting to serve in units commanded by the UN. I can understand why. The chain of command does not rest within the United States, and the military and civilian laws of the UN do not always match US laws.

ARTICLE 8 - THE STATE CONSTITUTIONAL REQUIREMENTS

This Article is pretty straight forward, with no sections or subsections. It is intended to make the state constitutions more uniform than what they are under the United States. For instance, Louisiana is under Napoleonic Law, rather than the more common English Common Law of their neighboring states.

I also wanted to make sure that there were term limits for all elected officials. No one shall make a career out of serving in the government, or at least it should be more difficult for someone to do so. I just don't want the elected officials to forget what it is really like out there in the real world. Career politicians, in my opinion, have become insulated from society and reality.

The same restrictions on bills in Congress should also apply to bills in the state legislatures.

And, lastly, I wanted to protect the property owners that live outside of city limits by restricting how cities annex the lands around them. All too often, a city will try to grab as much land as it can, partly to increase revenues, but also to keep the city from being surrounded and locked in, or in other cases to block the growth of a rival community.

Dallas, Texas, found itself in that situation. It can't grow anywhere except up, because it is completely surrounded by smaller cities. And I see it more locally, too. But I didn't want the people living in those areas to lose their voice in the matter, either. Some folks just don't want to live in a city.

ARTICLE 9 - THE CONSTITUTIONAL AMENDMENT PROCESS

There shall be only one way to change the Constitution. That is through amendments. This article covers the three ways to propose an amendment, the one way to pass an amendment, and what happens to the amendment if it does not get passed.

The amendment can be proposed by two-thirds vote in both houses of Congress, or it can be proposed by the legislatures in two-thirds of the states in the Great Republic, or it can be proposed by popular vote of the citizens in two-thirds of the states.

These votes must be done within a one-year period. I did that because of what is going on with the Constitutional Convention. They are waiting for one or two more states to vote on it before they go forward with it. Never mind that it has been going on for several years now. What if some of those states changed their minds?

Once the amendment has been proposed, it shall take a two-thirds vote in the legislatures of two-thirds of the states to ratify it. If the amendment fails, then its proponents shall have to wait five years before they can try again.

ARTICLE 10 - THE RATIFICATION REQUIREMENT

It shall take a minimum of two states to adopt the Constitution of the Great Republic in order for the nation to be officially born. It does not matter which states. It could be a state from Canada and a state from Mexico. It could be a parish from France or a prefect from Japan. Or it could be two states from the United States of America. This system is designed to allow for many more states to join.

My one fear about this Constitution is that I may have inadvertently left holes in it that the corrupt could take and twist to their advantage. I have tried to tie up all the loose ends, plug the holes and lock things down to where it cannot be abused and misinterpreted, deliberately or otherwise.

CHAPTER 4

A PEACEFUL TRANSITION

"When in the Course of human events, it becomes necessary for one people to dissolve the political bands which have connected them with another, and to assume among the powers of the earth, the separate and equal station to which the Laws of Nature and of Nature's God entitle them, a decent respect to the opinions of mankind requires that they should declare the causes which impel them to the separation." Declaration of Independence, July 4, 1776

Words have meaning . . .
Secession - to withdraw from a political body, in this case, the United States of America.
Insurrection - a violent uprising against a government.

The Civil War was the last time any state attempted to secede from the Union, and I have heard it cited time and again that the Union victory was the reason why secession is "unconstitutional." Unfortunately for them, the Constitution of the United States of

America, including all twenty-seven amendments, does not mention secession at all! How can secession be "unconstitutional" when it does not even appear in the Constitution?

According to the Tenth Amendment, ratified on December 15, 1791, "The powers not delegated to the United States by the Constitution, nor prohibited by it to the States, are reserved to the States respectively, or to the people."

If secession is not a power delegated to the United States, nor prohibited by it to the states, then it is a power reserved to the states or to the people. There is no Constitutional Amendment declaring secession to be "unconstitutional," and the outcome of the Civil War did not change that fact.

Abraham Lincoln, in his Inaugural Address in March of 1861, declared the secession of South Carolina, Mississippi, Florida, Alabama, Georgia, Louisiana, and Texas, to be an unconstitutional attempt to dissolve the Union. Again, there is no power granted to the Federal Government that prevents the dissolution of the Union. "Honest Abe" was wrong on that matter, but I see another flaw in his argument. Those States were not dissolving the Union. They were severing all ties to it. The United States of America would still be intact, but without those seven states.

Lincoln looked at the United States Constitution as a contract that all participants signed. Lincoln stressed that states wishing to secede must get "permission" from all the other states to do so, but that is not how the original thirteen colonies joined the union. Each one adopted the Constitution in its own time. They didn't get together as a group to do so, either. And they didn't get permission from the other states to join.

It was only later that new states being formed needed permission from the United States Congress. Sure, you need permission to join, but why do you need permission to leave? Why should one state get a say in whether or not another state leaves? I would say that the other states would not have "standing," to borrow a term from the legal system. To prevent a state from seceding is being a bully at best, a jailer at worst, with the state "imprisoned" in a country they no longer respect.

Lincoln used his oath of office, "to preserve, protect, and defend the United States Constitution" as an excuse to "preserve the union," but that is not what the oath said. It said to preserve, protect, and defend the Constitution! The president is to uphold the Constitution! It says nothing about keeping states from seceding, a power I have already stated that the Constitution and Federal Government has no power over!

Had Lincoln any respect for the Constitution he was sworn to uphold, he would have allowed these states to vote on secession in a peaceful manner and if they voted to leave, then he should have wished them well. Instead, Lincoln's stance on secession made the use of force inevitable. On a side note, if Lincoln had any respect for the Constitution, he would not have suspended habeas corpus during the Civil War!

As of January 29, 1861, there were thirty-four states in the Union. With the secession of seven states, and later, another four states, that left twenty-three in the Union, not counting territories in the west. The war between the states, to me, was a glaring statement that the United States was still intact! It was not dissolved!

Nothing since then has changed! Secession is still a power held by the states and the people! There is no basis in the Constitution of the United States to prevent states from leaving. Period. Only through the violence of the Civil War was the Union "preserved." It is like a bully telling his victim, "I beat you up, so that means you can't leave me!" In other words, "MIGHT MAKES RIGHT!" Even our own "Pledge of Allegiance" perpetuates the myth that secession is impossible, with the words, "...one nation, indivisible..."

By saying that a state cannot "dissolve the union," you are saying that states have entered into an irrevocable contract. But, according to Merriam-Webster, irrevocable means "impossible to revoke," and it means "unchangeable." If it is unchangeable, then we have to disregard all the amendments passed since then, including the 13th, 14th, and 15th amendments. The Constitution has been changed, so it is not irrevocable.

Secession can be done in a peaceful manner, if the United States government does nothing to stop it. If the United States government decides to use force, then war will be inevitable. I personally don't believe the United States will willingly allow any state to secede, because like all tyrants, they fear losing their power, and they will use any means they deem necessary to prevent it from happening. But the government could be persuaded, and I'll tell you how.

First, I would take the media by storm, a media blitz outlining the reasons for secession, and the reasons it is NOT unconstitutional. I would tell the whole world that it is a peaceful secession, unless the United States government uses force to prevent it. I would also remind the world that the United States of America is not being dissolved, it is still intact, only diminished in population, resources, and status.

Second, I would refrain from voting to secede until I had something with which to replace the United States Constitution. South Carolina had nothing prepared to take the place of the US government when they seceded. In fact, there was no Confederate Constitution for three months after South Carolina seceded.

I have examined the Constitution of the Confederate States of America and I found it wanting. It looked like they had taken the United States Constitution and scribbled on it! It was so bad that nothing in there made it to the Constitution of the Great Republic. But I digress. The purpose of the Constitution of the Great Republic was to have something well thought out and prepared for such an eventuality. So the vote to secede should be accompanied by a vote to adopt the Constitution of the Great Republic.

After the first two states secede and adopt this Constitution, I would then go to the United Nations and petition them to recognize these two states as an independent nation. We must make a strong case for independence to the people of the world. If enough nations recognize the formation of the Great Republic, that would go a long way toward securing a peaceful secession.

I want to make the case to the world that the United States shall continue to exist, that it is not being "dissolved." For me, that is very important. I want the United States to continue on, to exist, so that it will remain saddled with all the debt it has taken "in my name." I don't want the Great Republic to take any debt the United States has accrued. I could change my mind on that issue if, and only if, the United States voluntarily relinquishes all holdings within the seceding states, including, but not limited to, military bases and equipment, including weapons, ammunition, tanks, aircraft, and ships. If the United States decides to use force to prevent secession, then those bases and vehicles and equipment will be forfeited to the Great Republic, and they can keep their debt.

One thing that I would insist upon, when voting to secede and whether or not to adopt the Constitution of the Great Republic, is that only citizens of the state be allowed to vote, and they must prove their identity through government-issued cards that include their picture.

There will be cries of "racism" and "discrimination against the elderly and the poor" who "can't afford picture identification cards," but those arguments are bogus. The poor have cards. They have to have them in order to obtain their benefits, and to get a lot of other things. Photo ID cards are not discriminatory if everyone must show one. For those who "don't have a vehicle" to go get a picture ID, my answer is this, activists currently bus them to the polls; they have friends and they have family to take them. Therefore, these same activists can take them to get their IDs.

If all goes well, the next step would be to call everyone home—all the members of the United States Congress, everyone in the United States armed forces, and so on. No one should be forced to come and no one should be prohibited from returning or leaving.

New elections should be held, to elect the members of the new Congress, and a new president. A new Supreme Court should also be appointed as soon as possible, too. A primary concern would be to quickly form the new armed forces, the Republic Marines. I know there will be a lot of work to be done at this point, and I hope to give ideas on some of the topics.

I would give those who do not wish to join the Great Republic, who wish to remain United States citizens, and all illegal immigrants, thirty days to either receive their "alien" cards or to leave. All those who are in the territory illegally after that will be deported and their nation of origin will be billed for the cost, regardless of where they came from.

Next, I would like people to create charities, specifically charities to take over the benefits granted by Social Security, Medicare, and Medicaid, as these programs will be ended under the new government. If these programs are so great, then why not make participation in them voluntary? Why not make contributing to them voluntary?

There are, figuratively, a million things to do in order to form the Great Republic, and one of them concerns the laws of the land. I hate to say it, but I think I would keep all the laws that have been passed so far and let the new Congress start repealing them at their own pace. I don't want to have criminals say to themselves that there are no laws when the Great Republic is established, and that they can commit whatever crime they want because "there are no laws against it" yet.

Another option would be to have the current laws remain on the books for thirty days before being automatically repealed. The new Congress would have a brief window in order to pass new laws before they are gone.

A third option would be to set up a committee to review all the current laws and recommend which ones to keep and which to repeal during the period of time between adoption of the Constitution and the swearing in of the new Congress, president, and Supreme Court.

Lastly, I wanted to mention the following ideas. They cannot properly be part of the Constitution itself, but I would be interested in seeing them implemented in the Great Republic:

(1) I hate having to change the clocks every spring, losing an hour of sleep. It feels like jet lag. If I had my way, we would stay on Standard Time year-round. I would even go so far as to even out where the time zones are located. For example, Michigan is in the Eastern Time Zone while Alabama, which is due south of that state, is in the Central Time Zone. They should both be in one time zone or the other.

(2) The right to protest goes hand in hand with freedom of speech and freedom of assembly, but I would add one thing that it does not include. Protesters do not have the right to block streets or access to homes, businesses or government buildings, or the right to harass those entering or exiting them. That said, government, corporations, unions, organizations and people do not have the right to create "free speech zones" as the entire country is a free speech zone.

Protesters should respect the rights of others and the laws. Littering, and public urination and defecation are unacceptable. Shouting and the use of bullhorns are acceptable, except between the hours of nine in the evening to nine the following morning in residential areas. Rioting, looting, and destroying the property of others are unacceptable forms of protest.

(3) All voting machines shall use sixty-five pound cardstock ballots, with all names and positions printed on them. No electronic machines shall be used.

Each machine shall be numbered and shall imprint its number on every ballot a voter inserts into it. Each machine shall keep a running tally of the number of votes cast and shall print the number of each vote on each ballot. It should also print the precinct number. So it will print something like Precinct 28, Machine 5, Ballot 281 on one ballot and Precinct 28, Machine 5, Ballot 282 on the next one, and so forth.

When the polling place closes in the evening, those who monitor the voting process shall go to each machine and record how many ballots were cast on it, so that when the time comes to tally the votes, they can verify that the number of ballots cast equals the number of voters. This is to prevent fraud. It would also go a long way in the investigation in the "discovery" of "additional ballots" that we sometimes hear about.

No one, not even those who run the polling place, and those who are observing, shall record which person uses which machine and what their number was. The numbering system is to be used only in tallying the votes, not to figure out who voted for which candidate.

Voters may examine their ballot before submitting it, to ensure the machine has not been tampered with and to remove any "hanging chads."

Upon exiting the voting booth, each voter shall have their left thumb, or appropriate digit if the thumb is missing, dipped in blue dye. This should keep people voting in one precinct from going to another and voting again, the proverbial "vote early and vote often." In the "old days," such measures weren't necessary because travel times and distance made it impractical, but these days, you can vote in New York and then fly to Lost (sic on purpose) Angeles and vote there.

Citizens of the Great Republic living in other countries may vote in the consulate, or if they are serving in the military, at a polling place on their base or ship at sea. All too often those serving in the military have had their absentee ballots shipped late, or if they arrived on time, shipped home too late, or have had them tossed on one technicality or other.

(4) I am currently on the fence as to whether or not to allow lobbyists. There is currently a lot of corruption

in that "profession." I would like to see at least a law that prohibits former members of Congress and their immediate families from being lobbyists, as it leads to a conflict of interest and cronyism.

(5) Birth certificates must show citizenship status of parents and child at the time of the child's birth.

(6) The so-called "separation of church and state" does not mean those employed by the government must give up their religious freedoms. Government employees expressing religious freedoms does not mean an endorsement or promotion of their religion. The government can put disclaimers on statements, much like that of advertisements and television shows, where the channel says that "the views expressed do not necessarily represent those of the station, staff, and management ..."

(7) Territorial waters extend to two hundred miles off the coast, or half the distance to another country, whichever is less. I also want the Great Republic to ignore any nation, or group of nations, which try to control the oceans, including the UN with their LOST treaty. And not to forget China, building islands in the ocean in order to claim more territory. That won't fly with me.

(8) Regarding the press, they should not publish the names of suspects in crimes. They should wait until after the trial and then report on the crime and name the one(s) convicted. By publishing the name of the suspect, it makes the suspect a victim if he or she is later found not guilty. That person has already been "convicted in the court of public opinion." And the

press' protest that they do print retractions rings false. At least until they start publishing the retractions in the same fashion as the original story, instead of burying it deep within the news. So, if the original story was front page news, so should the retraction be, in the same bold face type!

(9) As for law enforcement, I would like to see SWAT teams held in reserve, as backup to regular law enforcement, rather than as "front line" units. I also would like to see law enforcement officers undergo psychological evaluation every two years, and find ways for them to relieve the stress they are under. It is a dangerous job, and like infantry in combat, they need to be rotated out of the line from time to time. And lastly, I would like law enforcement officers to learn Aikido, to take down criminals without resorting to firearms, batons, pepper spray, or tasers.

(10) Any religion that practices slavery, that makes women second-class citizens or property, that makes infidels second-class citizens (third-class, or less), that says infidels must convert or be killed, that says it is okay to lie to, and lie about, infidels, that says we must have laws to prevent people from insulting other people's religion, that says it is okay to kill those who insult their religion, is not a religion allowed in the Great Republic. At least not until they have a REFORMATION to deal with these issues. I know I may get a lot of flack over this, but there are laws on the books. Slavery is currently unconstitutional, hence illegal, and women have the right to vote and own property; murder is

against the law, and there are laws against fraud and lying. Plus, any law that keeps people from insulting other people's religion is a violation of the freedom of speech. Nothing is said about being free from "insults" or free from being offended.

(11) I have heard the refrain, "You cannot legislate morality." That is an outright lie. Most, if not all, laws are based on morals. Laws against slavery, murder, stealing, lying. These are moral issues! If there were no moral laws, then this country would be worse than the "wild west," which actually wasn't as wild as the movies portray. It would descend into chaos, as people would move from one depravity to the next, each one worse than before.

(12) Regarding those who are in the armed forces of the United States and who wish to join the Great Republic, I would demand that the United States release them from their oaths and allow them to leave peacefully. These men and women should be allowed to join the Republic Marines and retain their current ranks.

The Republic Marines, being one branch, shall have one uniform and one ranking system. The uniforms shall have patches indicating where the soldier is serving, such as infantry, artillery, tank, aircraft pilot, maintenance, military police, and the like.

(13) Illegal immigration is a serious problem. I have seen where employers blackmail employees who are here illegally, threatening them with deportation, and I have seen illegals blackmail their employers, threatening

to report them to the authorities, as it is illegal to hire illegal aliens.

By definition, illegal immigrants are breaking the laws of the country, and to me that shows their disregard for our laws. If they disregard our laws, how can they respect our country? Illegal immigrants, by definition, are not "law-abiding." And calling them something other than illegal aliens does not negate the fact that they broke our immigration laws.

Regarding immigration, I would like the federal government to hire more people to process the visa applications in an effort to speed up the process. It should take less than two weeks to process a visa application. Then I want to reduce the cost of visas to make it more affordable. I want the cost to be no more than fifty dollars. Next, I want to allow more people to apply for visas. Lastly, I will tell everyone who is in the country illegally to go apply for a visa.

Six months after the above has been implemented, I would give a warning to those who are still in the country illegally to either get a visa or to leave, and give them three months to comply. After the three months are up, I would start cracking down on illegal immigrants. Those who are still here would then be rounded up, deported, and their home country billed for the expense. Their home country may refuse to pay, and they may refuse to take their people back. But the Great Republic may respond by banning all businesses from dealing with that country. I would also add that those being deported should never be allowed to return to this country. The Great Republic shall not be forced to take deportees back if their home country refuses to accept them.

Once the illegal immigration problem is dealt with, I want to make the process of naturalization smoother, more efficient, and affordable. It should not take more than one year for all the paperwork to be processed and the applicant vetted by background checks. And the fees should not be more than one hundred dollars.

I am all for immigration into the country, but I am very much against illegal immigration. I am also against allowing anyone and everyone into the country. For national sovereignty, the government must be allowed to set quotas on entry. Otherwise, what's the point of even having borders?

(14) A new flag needs to be created. I would like it to be a navy blue square, about a meter on each side, with an eight point gold star in the center. With the star properly centered, you could fly the flag sideways, upside down or backwards and it would still look correct.

(15) Like a new flag, the Great Republic needs its own currency. I would like it to be composed of four coins and eight bank notes and known as Republic Dollars.

The first coin shall be the penny. The shape of the penny shall be octagonal, twenty millimeters in diameter, measured from corner to corner, not side to side, and one and one-half millimeters thick. It shall be made of polypropylene polymer and have the text "One Cent."

The second coin shall be the nickel. The shape of the nickel shall be round with a four millimeter by four millimeter square hole in the center. It shall be twenty millimeters in diameter and 1.5 millimeters thick. It shall be made of twenty-five percent nickel and seventy-five percent copper and have the text "Five Cents."

The third coin shall be the dime. The shape of the dime shall be octagonal. It shall be twenty-five millimeters in diameter, measured from corner to corner, not side to side, and two millimeters thick. It shall be made of brass and have the text "Ten Cents."

And the fourth coin shall be the quarter. The shape of the quarter shall be round. It shall be thirty millimeters in diameter and 2.5 millimeters thick. It shall be made of twenty-five percent nickel and seventy-five percent copper and have the text "Twenty-five Cents."

As for the bank notes, they shall be in denominations of 1, 5, 10, 20, 50, 100, 500 and 1,000 Republic Dollars, with similar anti-counterfeit measures as found on Australian bank notes. The bank notes shall be made of polypropylene polymer and shall be one hundred fifty millimeters long and sixty millimeters wide.

The coins and bank notes shall have their denominations in Braille for the blind, as well as the phrase "In God We Trust" on the obverse.

The cost to produce the currency, both coins and bank notes, shall not exceed half the value of the currency itself. With the creation of the Great Republic, I would want the exchange rate between the United States Dollar and the Republic Dollar to be on an equal basis, one dollar for one dollar.

(16) I would like to see the development of thorium-based nuclear reactors. From what I have read, they are smaller and cheaper to build and maintain than uranium-based reactors, the half-life of the waste product is measured in hundreds of years rather than tens of thousands, we have plenty of thorium available in the country, and thorium cannot be used to make nuclear weapons.

This country is dependent upon electricity and generating it should be a priority. I would also like to see the electrical infrastructure improved so that if there were a power failure in one area it would not cascade and take down other areas. Lastly, I would do away with the so-called "smart grid" idea. The power companies do not need to know our power consumption on a minute-by-minute basis. They sold us that bill of goods as a "convenience" to us, but it actually is a boon to them. They tell us that the system will alert them to power failures in our area, but phone calls from people in the dark will let them know just as quickly.

CHAPTER 5

ADDITIONAL THOUGHTS

SOCIALISM

I feel compelled to comment on socialism, or at least my understanding of it, especially in light of Bernie Sanders. He is a self-described democratic socialist. I wonder how much different democratic socialism is from National Socialists. You remember the National Socialists, don't you? They were Nazis! And didn't we have a war to defeat those people?

Socialism is defined as "a political and economic theory of social organization that advocates that the means of production, distribution, and exchange should be owned or regulated by the community as a whole." It is a stepping-stone to communism, which exchanges "should be owned or regulated" to "shall be owned."

Liberals want an end to poverty, healthcare for everyone, a much smaller wage gap, and no discrimination, among other noble-sounding ideas. They want to regulate the production, distribution, and exchange of goods and services to achieve their goals, which is a re-distribution of wealth, because the wealthy have and the poor have not. That is the only way they can "reduce the wage gap," "stop pollution," and all these other ideas.

They look at "owned or regulated by the community as a whole" benignly, but it actually means being owned or regulated by the government. They want state-compelled "compassion" so they can feel better about themselves. "See! I care!" No, you don't. You did nothing except have the people who thought, worked, and produced be forced to pay for programs you believe people "need, " whether they actually need them or not.

It sounds like some people are fine with a "little socialism" but socialism never stays little, and it never stays socialist for long. It soon turns into tyranny.

Look at the noble-sounding Environmental Protection Agency. They are re-defining "wetlands" in order to enhance their power, to increase the area they can tell people what they can and cannot do to their own property. The Affordable Care Act is designed to put the government in control over people's health. Once the government is paying for your health care, they can dictate how you live in order to reduce their costs.

Look at Nazi Germany. How many mentally impaired people were killed by their government and why? The "why" was easy. They saw the mentally impaired as a drain on their economy, a burden that did not contribute to the society, and threatened the "purity of the race," and so they were eliminated.

And what do we have that looks like that? The so-called "death panels" that the liberals vehemently decried as false. Strictly speaking, there are no "death panels, " but there are committees that go by different names that serve the same purpose. Aren't people over a certain age supposed to discuss "end of life options" with their doctors? It's "nuance."

With Hitler, it didn't take long for their elected government to descend into a tyranny. To unite the people with a common cause, they chose a group to "hate," the Jews, but they also had to silence the opposition. Not all Germans wanted socialism and the government had to use terror, coercion, and force to get them to step into line. They created the gestapo and used the SS to accomplish this task. Just remember that the Soviet Union and East Germany, and most of the other modern socialist/communist governments have secret police. THAT is what is in store for people who want socialist policies!

The problem with liberals is that they believe that all money and property belong to them and they are the government. That makes us subjects, instead of citizens. And it makes them tyrants.

The desire for socialism is based, I believe, on "utopia," which is an idea of a "perfect" world, where nothing bad happens, everything is orderly and neat and clean. No one is without a job. No one goes hungry, or is homeless. And no one is without health care.

Utopia is a myth. It can never be, at least here on Earth. Human nature prevents it. Human nature seeks to satisfy the self - "what's in it for me." A person will put as much effort into a job as the reward for completing it: The greater the reward, the greater the work; the less the reward, the less work. Why else would people do such dangerous jobs that pay much better than the average worker? Those seeking to create utopia only end up sowing misery and death. Ask those many millions of people who had to die for Mao's society.

So what is the solution? Use capitalism to generate the wealth and rely on charitable donations to help the poor, the homeless, etc. The United States has always been very giving, especially to charities.

Some might say that charities can't bring in enough money to pay for these things, but I argue that if the people have enough money to be taxed into giving, they have enough to charitably give. The difference in the Great Republic would be that they would finally have a choice in the matter. And who knows, they may donate even more, if given the choice.

THE (GLOBAL) GREAT REPUBLIC

After much thought, I realized that creating the Great Republic out of the United States could cause chaos, and potentially split or uproot families. It would be difficult for many people. What if there was a way to implement it without splitting the nation apart?

Originally, I had intended the Constitution of the Great Republic to grow, to incorporate states out of other nations, like British Columbia and Alberta from Canada, or Nuevo Leon and Tamaulipas from Mexico. But what if it could be more? What if it could take the place of, say, the United Nations?

I looked at the United Nations and thought to myself that it is making a lousy "World Government."

There is no representation of the people, and there are too many dictatorships involved. I don't like the fact that those who violate human rights are placed in charge of committees that investigate human rights violations.

The United States and other republics in the world are unequally yoked with tyrannies. The United Nations takes in money from member nations, but a majority of it comes from the United States, and we have little say in how it is used. Currently, there is plenty of fraud and waste in the United Nations.

And troops serving under the banner of the United Nations don't have a good reputation. Some have raped, and some have taken bribes. Some have looked the other way while atrocities are committed, atrocities they were supposed to be stopping.

Those in charge in the UN seem to want to create, with the Law of the Sea Treaty, a form of tax that would create a steady source of income, with no strings or controls attached. If that happens, then the UN will be self-funding and I fear it would then turn into a monster.

I have heard many people call for the United States to withdraw from the United Nations. But I think there should be something to replace it with, and so I considered using the Constitution of the Great Republic to do just that. There would be a few minor modifications to the Constitution that would need to be taken care of first.

One such modification would be in regards to the state governments. When the Constitution refers to states and state governments, it would need to be changed to nations and national governments. And the national, or federal, government, would need to be changed to something like the Global Government. So the United States would become a state under the Great Republic, and so would Japan, Mexico, and Canada, if they joined.

Another change would be regarding references to the Republic Dollar. I would be open to keeping it or going with something else, such as the Republic Peso, Republic Yen, Republic Pound, or Republic Mark. I could even go so far as to accept Republic Credits, though it may be copyrighted.

Also, for the House of Representatives, I would have one person for every five million citizens in the member nation, instead of six hundred thousand.

Of course, there are pros and cons to this plan, so I'll start with the cons.

First off, the Constitution of the Great Republic demands that all those who wish to join must have a republican form of government. This means that North Korea, China, Saudi Arabia, and the United Arab Emirates, for example, may not join until they have a new government.

Second, some of these other governments might get nervous about a new nation that spans the globe, especially if these other governments are tyrannies. They don't want their people seeing this new global nation, with its freedoms and prosperity. Their people might get ideas, like joining them.

Third, some countries might balk at joining the Great Republic out of fear of losing their identities. Take Japan, for example. They might fear losing their traditions and culture. They might fear being overrun with "foreigners," who will change everything. And they may not like the idea of English being the official language.

Some, or many, might also balk at the provisions in Article 6, regarding the right to bear arms, but if they realize that right is for self-protection, because the police don't stop crime in its tracks, and to prevent the government from turning into a dictatorship, then they might be more open to it. I should remind them that one reason why Japan didn't really consider invading the United States during World War II was the number of privately-held firearms, and the fact they would have to march on Washington DC to force our surrender. And to think that during hunting season in Wisconsin, there are more people out with rifles in that state than most countries have soldiers!

A less mildly offensive "con" would be the effect that joining the Great Republic would have regarding FIFA soccer and the Olympics. If those outside the Great Republic insist on having one team for FIFA, then simply withdraw from FIFA and create one between member nations, much like the National Football League's Super Bowl or the National Baseball League's World Series.

I do foresee the possibility of trouble with rogue elements, such as the mafia, yakuza, and drug cartels. The freedom of movement between nations may aid them in spreading to other areas of the world, but having law enforcement under a bigger roof might enable the police to track them easier, too.

Some nations might fear the United States dominating everything within the Great Republic, but there are other nations, like India, that might serve to counter-balance any influence the US might have. Besides, the checks and balances system is there to protect the minority from the rule of the majority. The Senate would provide equal footing, and migrations between member nations might change the dynamics altogether in the House of Representatives.

And now for the pros.

The Global Great Republic would be something akin to either the European Union or the British Commonwealth. Member nations would keep their identities, but be a part of something greater, with proper representation and accountability, and with proper checks and balances.

English is the official language, but not the only language. In Japan, documents would be written in Japanese and English. In Brazil, they would be in Portuguese and English. They would not be forced to give up their languages. Besides, English is currently the standard language for business in the world.

The United States is composed of individual states, and the Global Great Republic would be composed of individual nations. Like states, these nations would keep their traditions, their flags. They would just fly a new flag either above, or beside, their own, just like the states here.

If multiple nations adopt this Constitution, then people may travel freely between nations, leading to migrations, and tourism may simply explode. I know that I would love to go visit England and Japan, but I don't have a passport. No passports or permits would be required to travel to other member nations. It would also solve some of the illegal immigration problems, especially if the United States and Mexico both joined up.

Trade between member nations would also increase dramatically, as tariffs and trade agreements would no longer be an issue. The North American Free Trade Agreement could be thrown out, along with the Trans-Pacific Partnership. Industry could boom as corporations would be free to move from region to region. With a unified monetary system, money would be good everywhere within the Global Great Republic. So-called "third world" nations could see their economies and their standards of living improve.

It would allow the NFL, NBA, and MLB to spread to other areas of the world, and allow soccer to make greater inroads here. It would be a two-way street with teams being formed everywhere. It should make things entertaining, at least.

The freedoms created by joining the Global Great Republic would include information and technology, marketing and education, and teaching of history of other nations. Corporations and private individuals from member nations could also pool their resources for space exploration.

Another positive thing for joining the Global Great Republic, at least for a while, is the fact that there is no Democratic Party in Japan, no Republican Party in Mexico, no PRI Party in Germany, no PAN Party in Ireland, and so on. Unlike in the United States, where we have the two main parties controlling politics, and similar situations in other countries, they won't have the power or coordination to take over the Global Great Republic's political system. And with the checks on the flow of money and power, their ability to take over would be greatly restricted.

Alliances would go out the window! NATO and ANZUS would become defunct, assuming the members of these alliances all joined the Global Great Republic. The militaries of the member nations would be united under one uniform and one flag, and, more importantly, one chain of command.

I would love to see the following countries adopt the Constitution of the Global Great Republic: Andorra, Antigua and Barbuda, Argentina, Australia, Austria, Barbados, Belgium, Belize, Benin, Botswana, Brazil, Bulgaria, Canada, Cape Verde, Chile, Costa Rica, Croatia, Cyprus, Czech Republic, Denmark, Dominica, Dominican Republic, El Salvador, Estonia, Federated States of Micronesia, Finland, France, Germany, Ghana, Greece, Greenland, Guyana, Hungary, Iceland, India, Ireland, Israel, Italy, Jamaica, Japan, Kiribati, Latvia, Lesotho, Liechtenstein, Lithuania, Luxembourg, Malta, Marshall Islands, Mauritius, Monaco, Mongolia, Montenegro, Namibia, Nauru, Netherlands, New Zealand, Northern Cyprus, Norway,

Palau, Panama, Peru, Poland, Portugal, Puerto Rico, Romania, Saint Kitts and Nevis, Saint Lucia, Saint Vincent and the Grenadines, Samoa, San Marino, São Tomé and Príncipe, Senegal, Serbia, Slovakia, Slovenia, South Africa, South Korea, Spain, Suriname, Sweden, Switzerland, Taiwan, The Bahamas, Tonga, Trinidad and Tobago, Tuvalu, United Kingdom, United States, Uruguay, Vanuatu, and Vatican City. These nations were listed in Freedom House as "Free" nations. (freedomhouse.org/report/freedom-world/freedom-world-2014)

I was astonished to see Mexico listed as "partially free," and Russia listed as "not free." Ideally, I would love to see both of them join. I would love to see China join. In fact, I would love to see all nations of the world adopt this Constitution and join the Global Great Republic. But I fear many of them would never want to join. Their leaders, for one thing, who fear losing power, would be loathe to do so. But I can still hope.

CHAPTER 6

THE CONSTITUTION OF THE UNITED STATES OF AMERICA

PREAMBLE

We the People of the United States, in Order to form a more perfect Union, establish Justice, insure domestic Tranquility, provide for the common defense, promote the general Welfare, and secure the Blessings of Liberty to ourselves and our Posterity, do ordain and establish this Constitution for the United States of America.

ARTICLE I

SECTION 1

All legislative Powers herein granted shall be vested in a Congress of the United States, which shall consist of a Senate and House of Representatives.

SECTION 2

The House of Representatives shall be composed of Members chosen every second Year by the

People of the several States, and the Electors in each State shall have the Qualifications requisite for Electors of the most numerous Branch of the State Legislature.

No Person shall be a Representative who shall not have attained to the Age of twenty five Years, and been seven Years a Citizen of the United States, and who shall not, when elected, be an Inhabitant of that State in which he shall be chosen.

(Representatives and direct Taxes shall be apportioned among the several States which may be included within this Union, according to their respective Numbers, which shall be determined by adding to the whole Number of free Persons, including those bound to Service for a Term of Years, and excluding Indians not taxed, three fifths of all other Persons.) (The previous sentence in parentheses was modified by the 14th Amendment, section 2.) The actual Enumeration shall be made within three Years after the first Meeting of the Congress of the United States, and within every subsequent Term of ten Years, in such Manner as they shall by Law direct. The Number of Representatives shall not exceed one for every thirty Thousand, but each State shall have at Least one Representative; and until such enumeration shall be made, the State of New Hampshire shall be entitled to choose three, Massachusetts eight, Rhode Island and Providence Plantations one, Connecticut five, New York six, New Jersey four, Pennsylvania eight, Delaware one, Maryland six, Virginia ten, North Carolina five, South Carolina five and Georgia three.

When vacancies happen in the Representation from any State, the Executive Authority thereof shall issue Writs of Election to fill such Vacancies. The House of Representatives shall choose their Speaker and other Officers; and shall have the sole Power of Impeachment.

SECTION 3

The Senate of the United States shall be composed of two Senators from each State, (chosen by the Legislature thereof,) (The preceding words in parentheses superseded by 17th Amendment, section 1.) for six Years; and each Senator shall have one Vote.

Immediately after they shall be assembled in Consequence of the first Election, they shall be divided as equally as may be into three Classes. The Seats of the Senators of the first Class shall be vacated at the Expiration of the second Year, of the second Class at the Expiration of the fourth Year, and of the third Class at the Expiration of the sixth Year, so that one third may be chosen every second Year; (and if Vacancies happen by Resignation, or otherwise, during the Recess of the Legislature of any State, the Executive thereof may make temporary Appointments until the next Meeting of the Legislature, which shall then fill such Vacancies.) (The preceding words in parentheses were superseded by the 17th Amendment, section 2.)

No person shall be a Senator who shall not have attained to the Age of thirty Years, and been nine Years a Citizen of the United States, and who shall not, when elected, be an Inhabitant of that State for which he shall be chosen.

The Vice President of the United States shall be President of the Senate, but shall have no Vote, unless they be equally divided.

The Senate shall choose their other Officers, and also a President pro tempore, in the Absence of the Vice President, or when he shall exercise the Office of President of the United States.

The Senate shall have the sole Power to try all Impeachments. When sitting for that Purpose, they shall be on Oath or Affirmation. When the President of the United States is tried, the Chief Justice shall preside: And no Person shall be convicted without the Concurrence of two thirds of the Members present.

Judgment in Cases of Impeachment shall not extend further than to removal from Office, and disqualification to hold and enjoy any Office of honor, Trust or Profit under the United States: but the Party convicted shall nevertheless be liable and subject to Indictment, Trial, Judgment and Punishment, according to Law.

SECTION 4

The Times, Places and Manner of holding Elections for Senators and Representatives, shall be prescribed in each State by the Legislature thereof; but the Congress may at any time by Law make or alter such Regulations, except as to the Place of Choosing Senators.

The Congress shall assemble at least once in every Year, and such Meeting shall (be on the first Monday in December,) (The preceding words in parentheses were superseded by the 20th Amendment, section 2.) unless they shall by Law appoint a different Day.

SECTION 5

Each House shall be the Judge of the Elections, Returns and Qualifications of its own Members, and a Majority of each shall constitute a Quorum to do Business; but a smaller Number may adjourn from day to day, and may be authorized to compel the Attendance of absent Members, in such Manner, and under such Penalties as each House may provide.

Each House may determine the Rules of its Proceedings, punish its Members for disorderly Behavior, and, with the Concurrence of two-thirds, expel a Member.

Each House shall keep a Journal of its Proceedings, and from time to time publish the same, excepting such Parts as may in their Judgment require Secrecy; and the Yeas and Nays of the Members of either House on any question shall, at the Desire of one fifth of those Present, be entered on the Journal.

Neither House, during the Session of Congress, shall, without the Consent of the other, adjourn for more than three days, nor to any other Place than that in which the two Houses shall be sitting.

SECTION 6

(The Senators and Representatives shall receive a Compensation for their Services, to be ascertained by Law, and paid out of the Treasury of the United States.) (The preceding words in parentheses were modified by the 27th Amendment.) They shall in all Cases, except Treason, Felony and Breach of the Peace, be privileged from Arrest during their Attendance at the Session of their respective Houses, and in going to and returning from the same; and for any Speech or Debate in either House, they shall not be questioned in any other Place.

No Senator or Representative shall, during the Time for which he was elected, be appointed to any civil Office under the Authority of the United States which shall have been created, or the Emoluments whereof shall have been increased during such time; and no Person holding any Office under the United States, shall be a Member of either House during his Continuance in Office.

SECTION 7

All Bills for raising Revenue shall originate in the House of Representatives; but the Senate may propose or concur with Amendments as on other Bills.

Every Bill which shall have passed the House of Representatives and the Senate, shall, before it become a Law, be presented to the President of the United States; If he approve he shall sign it, but if not he shall return it, with his Objections to that House in which it shall have originated, who shall enter the Objections at large on their Journal, and proceed to reconsider it. If after such Reconsideration two thirds of that House shall agree to pass the Bill, it shall be sent, together with the Objections, to the other House, by which it shall likewise be reconsidered, and if approved by two thirds of that House, it shall become a Law. But in all such Cases the Votes of both Houses shall be determined by Yeas and Nays, and the Names of the Persons voting for and against the Bill shall be entered on the Journal of each House respectively. If any Bill shall not be returned by the President within ten Days (Sundays excepted) after it shall have been presented to him, the Same shall be a Law, in like Manner as if he had signed it, unless the Congress by their Adjournment prevent its Return, in which Case it shall not be a Law.

Every Order, Resolution, or Vote to which the Concurrence of the Senate and House of Representatives may be necessary (except on a question of Adjournment) shall be presented to the President of the United States; and before the Same shall take Effect, shall be approved by him, or being disapproved by him, shall be repassed by two thirds of the Senate and House of Representatives, according to the Rules and Limitations prescribed in the Case of a Bill.

SECTION 8

The Congress shall have Power To lay and collect Taxes, Duties, Imposts and Excises, to pay the Debts and provide for the common Defense and general Welfare of the United States; but all Duties, Imposts and Excises shall be uniform throughout the United States;

To borrow Money on the credit of the United States;

To regulate Commerce with foreign Nations, and among the several States, and with the Indian Tribes;

To establish an uniform Rule of Naturalization, and uniform Laws on the subject of Bankruptcies throughout the United States;

To coin Money, regulate the Value thereof, and of foreign Coin, and fix the Standard of Weights and Measures;

To provide for the Punishment of counterfeiting the Securities and current Coin of the United States;

To establish Post Offices and post Roads;

To promote the Progress of Science and useful Arts, by securing for limited Times to Authors and Inventors the exclusive Right to their respective Writings and Discoveries;

To constitute Tribunals inferior to the supreme Court;

To define and punish Piracies and Felonies committed on the high Seas, and Offenses against the Law of Nations;

To declare War, grant Letters of Marque and Reprisal, and make Rules concerning Captures on Land and Water;

To raise and support Armies, but no Appropriation of Money to that Use shall be for a longer Term than two Years;

To provide and maintain a Navy;

To make Rules for the Government and Regulation of the land and naval Forces;

To provide for calling forth the Militia to execute the Laws of the Union, suppress Insurrections and repel Invasions;

To provide for organizing, arming, and disciplining the Militia, and for governing such Part of them as may be employed in the Service of the United States, reserving to the States respectively, the Appointment of the Officers, and the Authority of training the Militia according to the discipline prescribed by Congress;

To exercise exclusive Legislation in all Cases whatsoever, over such District (not exceeding ten Miles square) as may, by Cession of particular States, and the Acceptance of Congress, become the Seat of the Government of the United States, and to exercise like Authority over all Places purchased by the Consent of the Legislature of the State in which the Same shall be, for the Erection of Forts, Magazines, Arsenals, dock-Yards, and other needful Buildings; And

To make all Laws which shall be necessary and proper for carrying into Execution the foregoing Powers, and all other Powers vested by this Constitution in the Government of the United States, or in any Department or Officer thereof.

SECTION 9

The Migration or Importation of such Persons as any of the States now existing shall think proper to admit, shall not be prohibited by the Congress prior to the Year one thousand eight hundred and eight, but a Tax or duty may be imposed on such Importation, not exceeding ten dollars for each Person.

The Privilege of the Writ of Habeas Corpus shall not be suspended, unless when in Cases of Rebellion or Invasion the public Safety may require it.

No Bill of Attainder or ex post facto Law shall be passed.

(No capitation, or other direct, Tax shall be laid, unless in Proportion to the Census or Enumeration herein before directed to be taken.) (Section in parentheses clarified by the 16th Amendment.)

No Tax or Duty shall be laid on Articles exported from any State.

No Preference shall be given by any Regulation of Commerce or Revenue to the Ports of one State over those of another: nor shall Vessels bound to, or from, one State, be obliged to enter, clear, or pay Duties in another.

No Money shall be drawn from the Treasury, but in Consequence of Appropriations made by Law; and a regular Statement and Account of the Receipts and Expenditures of all public Money shall be published from time to time.

No Title of Nobility shall be granted by the United States: And no Person holding any Office of Profit or Trust under them, shall, without the Consent of the Congress, accept of any present, Emolument, Office, or Title, of any kind whatever, from any King, Prince or foreign State.

SECTION 10

No State shall enter into any Treaty, Alliance, or Confederation; grant Letters of Marque and Reprisal; coin Money; emit Bills of Credit; make any Thing but gold and silver Coin a Tender in Payment of Debts; pass any Bill of Attainder, ex post facto Law, or Law impairing the Obligation of Contracts, or grant any Title of Nobility.

No State shall, without the Consent of the Congress, lay any Imposts or Duties on Imports or Exports, except what may be absolutely necessary for executing its inspection Laws: and the net Produce of all Duties and Imposts, laid by any State on Imports or Exports, shall be for the Use of the Treasury of the United States; and all such Laws shall be subject to the Revision and Control of the Congress.

No State shall, without the Consent of Congress, lay any duty of Tonnage, keep Troops, or Ships of War in time of Peace, enter into any Agreement or Compact with another State, or with a foreign Power, or engage in War, unless actually invaded, or in such imminent Danger as will not admit of delay.

ARTICLE II

SECTION 1

The executive Power shall be vested in a President of the United States of America. He shall hold his Office during the Term of four Years, and, together with the Vice President chosen for the same Term, be elected, as follows:

Each State shall appoint, in such Manner as the Legislature thereof may direct, a Number of Electors, equal to the whole Number of Senators and Representatives to which the State may be entitled in the Congress: but no Senator or Representative, or Person holding an Office of Trust or Profit under the United States, shall be appointed an Elector.

(The Electors shall meet in their respective States, and vote by Ballot for two persons, of whom one at least shall not be an Inhabitant of the same State with themselves. And they shall make a List of all the Persons voted for, and of the Number of Votes for each; which List they shall sign and certify, and transmit sealed to the Seat of the Government of the United States, directed to the President of the Senate. The President of the Senate shall, in the Presence of the Senate and House of Representatives, open all the Certificates, and the Votes shall then be counted. The Person having the greatest Number of Votes shall be the President, if such Number be a Majority of the whole Number of Electors appointed; and if there be more than one who have such Majority, and have an equal Number of Votes, then the House of Representatives shall immediately choose by Ballot one of them for President; and if no Person have a Majority, then from the five highest on the List the said House shall in like Manner choose the President. But in choosing the President, the Votes shall be taken by States, the Representation from each State having one Vote; a quorum for this Purpose shall consist of a Member or Members from two-thirds of the States, and a Majority of all the States shall be necessary to a Choice. In every Case, after the Choice of the President, the Person having the greatest Number of Votes of the Electors shall be the Vice President. But if there should remain two or more who have equal Votes, the Senate shall choose from them by Ballot the

Vice-President.) (This clause in parentheses was superseded by the 12th Amendment.)

The Congress may determine the Time of choosing the Electors, and the Day on which they shall give their Votes; which Day shall be the same throughout the United States.

No person except a natural born Citizen, or a Citizen of the United States, at the time of the Adoption of this Constitution, shall be eligible to the Office of President; neither shall any person be eligible to that Office who shall not have attained to the Age of thirty five Years, and been fourteen Years a Resident within the United States.

(In Case of the Removal of the President from Office, or of his Death, Resignation, or Inability to discharge the Powers and Duties of the said Office, the same shall devolve on the Vice President, and the Congress may by Law provide for the Case of Removal, Death, Resignation or Inability, both of the President and Vice President, declaring what Officer shall then act as President, and such Officer shall act accordingly, until the Disability be removed, or a President shall be elected.) (This clause in parentheses has been modified by the 20th and 25th Amendments.)

The President shall, at stated Times, receive for his Services, a Compensation, which shall neither be increased nor diminished during the Period for which he shall have been elected, and he shall not receive within that Period any other Emolument from the United States, or any of them.

Before he enter on the Execution of his Office, he shall take the following Oath or Affirmation: "I do solemnly swear (or affirm) that I will faithfully execute the Office of President of the United States, and will to the best of my Ability, preserve, protect and defend the Constitution of the United States."

SECTION 2

The President shall be Commander in Chief of the Army and Navy of the United States, and of the Militia of the several States, when called into the actual Service of the United States; he may require the Opinion, in writing, of the principal Officer in each of the executive Departments, upon any subject relating to the Duties of their respective Offices, and he shall have Power to Grant Reprieves and Pardons for Offenses against the United States, except in Cases of Impeachment.

He shall have Power, by and with the Advice and Consent of the Senate, to make Treaties, provided two thirds of the Senators present concur; and he shall nominate, and by and with the Advice and Consent of the Senate, shall appoint Ambassadors, other public Ministers and Consuls, Judges of the supreme Court, and all other Officers of the United States, whose

Appointments are not herein otherwise provided for, and which shall be established by Law: but the Congress may by Law vest the Appointment of such inferior Officers, as they think proper, in the President alone, in the Courts of Law, or in the Heads of Departments.

The President shall have Power to fill up all Vacancies that may happen during the Recess of the Senate, by granting Commissions which shall expire at the End of their next Session.

SECTION 3

He shall from time to time give to the Congress Information of the State of the Union, and recommend to their Consideration such Measures as he shall judge necessary and expedient; he may, on extraordinary Occasions, convene both Houses, or either of them, and in Case of Disagreement between them, with Respect to the Time of Adjournment, he may adjourn them to such Time as he shall think proper; he shall receive Ambassadors and other public Ministers; he shall take Care that the Laws be faithfully executed, and shall Commission all the Officers of the United States.

SECTION 4

The President, Vice President and all civil Officers of the United States, shall be removed from Office on Impeachment for, and Conviction of, Treason, Bribery, or other high Crimes and Misdemeanors.

ARTICLE III

SECTION 1

The judicial Power of the United States, shall be vested in one supreme Court, and in such inferior Courts as the Congress may from time to time ordain and establish. The Judges, both of the supreme and inferior Courts, shall hold their Offices during good Behavior, and shall, at stated Times, receive for their Services a Compensation, which shall not be diminished during their Continuance in Office.

SECTION 2

(The judicial Power shall extend to all Cases, in Law and Equity, arising under this Constitution, the Laws of the United States, and Treaties made, or which shall be made, under their Authority; to all Cases affecting Ambassadors, other public Ministers and Consuls; to all Cases of admiralty and maritime Jurisdiction; to Controversies to which the United States shall be a Party; to Controversies between two or more States; between a State and Citizens of another State; between Citizens of different States; between Citizens of the same State claiming Lands under Grants of different States, and between a State, or the Citizens thereof, and foreign States, Citizens or Subjects.) (This section in parentheses is modified by the 11th Amendment.)

In all Cases affecting Ambassadors, other public Ministers and Consuls, and those in which a State shall be Party, the supreme Court shall have original Jurisdiction. In all the other Cases before mentioned, the supreme Court shall have appellate Jurisdiction, both as to Law and Fact, with such Exceptions, and under such Regulations as the Congress shall make.

The Trial of all Crimes, except in Cases of Impeachment, shall be by Jury; and such Trial shall be held in the State where the said Crimes shall have been committed; but when not committed within any State, the Trial shall be at such Place or Places as the Congress may by Law have directed.

SECTION 3

Treason against the United States, shall consist only in levying War against them, or in adhering to their Enemies, giving them Aid and Comfort. No Person shall be convicted of Treason unless on the Testimony of two Witnesses to the same overt Act, or on Confession in open Court.

The Congress shall have power to declare the Punishment of Treason, but no Attainder of Treason shall work Corruption of Blood, or Forfeiture except during the Life of the Person attainted.

ARTICLE IV

SECTION 1

Full Faith and Credit shall be given in each State to the public Acts, Records, and judicial Proceedings of every other State. And the Congress may by general Laws prescribe the Manner in which such Acts, Records and Proceedings shall be proved, and the Effect thereof.

SECTION 2

The Citizens of each State shall be entitled to all Privileges and Immunities of Citizens in the several States.

A Person charged in any State with Treason, Felony, or other Crime, who shall flee from Justice, and be found in another State, shall on Demand of the executive Authority of the State from which he fled, be delivered up, to be removed to the State having Jurisdiction of the Crime.

(No Person held to Service or Labor in one State, under the Laws thereof, escaping into another, shall, in Consequence of any Law or Regulation therein, be discharged from such Service or Labor, But shall be delivered up on Claim of the Party to whom such Service or Labor may be due.) (This clause in parentheses is superseded by the 13th Amendment.)

SECTION 3

New States may be admitted by the Congress into this Union; but no new State shall be formed or erected within the Jurisdiction of any other State; nor any State be formed by the Junction of two or more States, or Parts of States, without the Consent of the Legislatures of the States concerned as well as of the Congress.

The Congress shall have Power to dispose of and make all needful Rules and Regulations respecting the Territory or other Property belonging to the United States; and nothing in this Constitution shall be so construed as to Prejudice any Claims of the United States, or of any particular State.

SECTION 4

The United States shall guarantee to every State in this Union a Republican Form of Government, and shall protect each of them against Invasion; and on Application of the Legislature, or of the Executive (when the Legislature cannot be convened) against domestic Violence.

ARTICLE V

The Congress, whenever two thirds of both Houses shall deem it necessary, shall propose Amendments to this Constitution, or, on the Application of the Legislatures of two thirds of the several States, shall call a Convention for proposing Amendments, which, in either Case, shall be valid to all Intents and Purposes, as Part of this Constitution, when ratified by the Legislatures of three fourths of the several States, or by Conventions in three fourths thereof, as the one or the other Mode of Ratification may be proposed by the Congress; Provided that no Amendment which may be made prior to the Year One thousand eight hundred and eight shall in any Manner affect the first and fourth Clauses in the Ninth Section of the first Article; and that no State, without its Consent, shall be deprived of its equal Suffrage in the Senate.

ARTICLE VI

All Debts contracted and Engagements entered into, before the Adoption of this Constitution, shall be as valid against the United States under this Constitution, as under the Confederation.

This Constitution, and the Laws of the United States which shall be made in Pursuance thereof; and all Treaties made, or which shall be made, under the Authority of the United States, shall be the supreme Law of the Land; and the Judges in every State shall be bound thereby, any Thing in the Constitution or Laws of any State to the Contrary notwithstanding.

The Senators and Representatives before mentioned, and the Members of the several State Legislatures, and all executive and judicial Officers, both of the United States and of the several States, shall be bound by Oath or

Affirmation, to support this Constitution; but no religious Test shall ever be required as a Qualification to any Office or public Trust under the United States.

ARTICLE VII

The Ratification of the Conventions of nine States, shall be sufficient for the Establishment of this Constitution between the States so ratifying the Same.

Done in Convention by the Unanimous Consent of the States present the Seventeenth Day of September in the Year of our Lord one thousand seven hundred and Eighty seven and of the Independence of the United States of America the Twelfth In Witness whereof We have hereunto subscribed our Names,

Go. Washington - President and deputy from Virginia

New Hampshire - John Langdon, Nicholas Gilman

Massachusetts - Nathaniel Gorham, Rufus King

Connecticut - Wm Saml Johnson, Roger Sherman

New York - Alexander Hamilton

New Jersey - Wil Livingston, David Brearley, Wm Paterson, Jona. Dayton

Pensylvania - B Franklin, Thomas Mifflin, Robt Morris, Geo. Clymer, Thos FitzSimons, Jared Ingersoll, James Wilson, Gouv Morris

Delaware - Geo. Read, Gunning Bedford jun,

John Dickinson, Richard Bassett, Jaco. Broom
Maryland - James McHenry, Dan of St Thos.
Jenifer, Danl Carroll
Virginia - John Blair, James Madison Jr.
North Carolina - Wm Blount, Richd Dobbs
Spaight, Hu Williamson
South Carolina - J. Rutledge, Charles Cotesworth
Pinckney, Charles Pinckney, Pierce Butler
Georgia - William Few, Abr Baldwin
Attest: William Jackson, Secretary

CHAPTER 7

AMENDMENTS TO THE US CONSTITUTION

The following are the Amendments to the Constitution. The first ten Amendments collectively are commonly known as the Bill of Rights.

AMENDMENT 1 - RATIFIED 12/15/1791.

Congress shall make no law respecting an establishment of religion, or prohibiting the free exercise thereof; or abridging the freedom of speech, or of the press; or the right of the people peaceably to assemble, and to petition the Government for a redress of grievances.

AMENDMENT 2 - RATIFIED 12/15/1791.

A well regulated Militia, being necessary to the security of a free State, the right of the people to keep and bear Arms, shall not be infringed.

AMENDMENT 3 - RATIFIED 12/15/1791.

No Soldier shall, in time of peace be quartered in any house, without the consent of the Owner, nor in time of war, but in a manner to be prescribed by law.

AMENDMENT 4 - RATIFIED 12/15/1791.

The right of the people to be secure in their persons, houses, papers, and effects, against unreasonable searches and seizures, shall not be violated, and no Warrants shall issue, but upon probable cause, supported by Oath or affirmation, and particularly describing the place to be searched, and the persons or things to be seized.

AMENDMENT 5 - RATIFIED 12/15/1791.

No person shall be held to answer for a capital, or otherwise infamous crime, unless on a presentment or indictment of a Grand Jury, except in cases arising in the land or naval forces, or in the Militia, when in actual service in time of War or public danger; nor shall any person be subject for the same offense to be twice put in jeopardy of life or limb; nor shall be compelled in any criminal case to be a witness against himself, nor be deprived of life, liberty, or property, without due process of law; nor shall private property be taken for public use, without just compensation.

AMENDMENT 6 - RATIFIED 12/15/1791.

In all criminal prosecutions, the accused shall enjoy the right to a speedy and public trial, by an impartial jury of the State and district wherein the crime shall have been committed, which district shall have been previously ascertained by law, and to be informed of the nature and cause of the accusation; to be confronted with the witnesses against him; to have compulsory process for obtaining witnesses in his favor, and to have the Assistance of Counsel for his defense.

AMENDMENT 7 - RATIFIED 12/15/1791.

In Suits at common law, where the value in controversy shall exceed twenty dollars, the right of trial by jury shall be preserved, and no fact tried by a jury, shall be otherwise re-examined in any Court of the United States, than according to the rules of the common law.

AMENDMENT 8 - RATIFIED 12/15/1791.

Excessive bail shall not be required, nor excessive fines imposed, nor cruel and unusual punishments inflicted.

AMENDMENT 9 - RATIFIED 12/15/1791.

The enumeration in the Constitution, of certain rights, shall not be construed to deny or disparage others retained by the people.

AMENDMENT 10 - RATIFIED 12/15/1791.

The powers not delegated to the United States by the Constitution, nor prohibited by it to the States, are reserved to the States respectively, or to the people.

AMENDMENT 11 - RATIFIED 2/7/1795.

The Judicial power of the United States shall not be construed to extend to any suit in law or equity, commenced or prosecuted against one of the United States by Citizens of another State, or by Citizens or Subjects of any Foreign State.

AMENDMENT 12 - RATIFIED 6/15/1804.

The Electors shall meet in their respective states, and vote by ballot for President and Vice-President, one of whom, at least, shall not be an inhabitant of the same state with themselves; they shall name in their ballots the person voted for as President, and in distinct ballots the person voted for as Vice-President, and they shall make distinct lists of all persons voted for as President, and of all persons voted for as Vice-President and of the number of votes for each, which lists they shall sign and certify, and transmit sealed to the seat of the government of the United States, directed to the President of the Senate;

The President of the Senate shall, in the presence of the Senate and House of Representatives, open all the certificates and the votes shall then be counted;

The person having the greatest Number of votes for President, shall be the President, if such number be a majority of the whole number of Electors appointed; and if no person have such majority, then from the persons having the highest numbers not exceeding three on the list of those voted for as President, the House of Representatives shall choose immediately, by ballot, the President. But in choosing the President, the votes shall be taken by states, the representation from each state having one vote; a quorum for this purpose shall consist of a member or members from two-thirds of the states, and a majority of all the states shall be necessary to a choice. And if the House of Representatives shall not choose a President whenever the right of choice shall devolve upon them, before the fourth day of

March next following, then the Vice-President shall act as President, as in the case of the death or other constitutional disability of the President.

The person having the greatest number of votes as Vice-President, shall be the Vice-President, if such number be a majority of the whole number of Electors appointed, and if no person have a majority, then from the two highest numbers on the list, the Senate shall choose the Vice-President; a quorum for the purpose shall consist of two-thirds of the whole number of Senators, and a majority of the whole number shall be necessary to a choice. But no person constitutionally ineligible to the office of President shall be eligible to that of Vice-President of the United States.

AMENDMENT 13 - RATIFIED 12/6/1865.

1. Neither slavery nor involuntary servitude, except as a punishment for crime whereof the party shall have been duly convicted, shall exist within the United States, or any place subject to their jurisdiction.

2. Congress shall have power to enforce this article by appropriate legislation.

AMENDMENT 14 - RATIFIED 7/9/1868.

1. All persons born or naturalized in the United States, and subject to the jurisdiction thereof, are citizens of the United States and of the State wherein they reside. No State shall make or enforce any law which shall abridge the privileges or immunities of citizens of the United States; nor shall any State deprive any

person of life, liberty, or property, without due process of law; nor deny to any person within its jurisdiction the equal protection of the laws.

2. Representatives shall be apportioned among the several States according to their respective numbers, counting the whole number of persons in each State, excluding Indians not taxed. But when the right to vote at any election for the choice of electors for President and Vice-President of the United States, Representatives in Congress, the Executive and Judicial officers of a State, or the members of the Legislature thereof, is denied to any of the male inhabitants of such State, being twenty-one years of age, and citizens of the United States, or in any way abridged, except for participation in rebellion, or other crime, the basis of representation therein shall be reduced in the proportion which the number of such male citizens shall bear to the whole number of male citizens twenty-one years of age in such State.

3. No person shall be a Senator or Representative in Congress, or elector of President and Vice-President, or hold any office, civil or military, under the United States, or under any State, who, having previously taken an oath, as a member of Congress, or as an officer of the United States, or as a member of any State legislature, or as an executive or judicial officer of any State, to support the Constitution of the United States, shall have engaged in insurrection or rebellion against the same, or given aid or comfort to the enemies thereof. But Congress may by a vote of two-thirds of each House, remove such disability.

4. The validity of the public debt of the United States, authorized by law, including debts incurred for payment of pensions and bounties for services in suppressing insurrection or rebellion, shall not be questioned. But neither the United States nor any State shall assume or pay any debt or obligation incurred in aid of insurrection or rebellion against the United States, or any claim for the loss or emancipation of any slave; but all such debts, obligations and claims shall be held illegal and void.

5. The Congress shall have power to enforce, by appropriate legislation, the provisions of this article.

AMENDMENT 15 - RATIFIED 2/3/1870.

1. The right of citizens of the United States to vote shall not be denied or abridged by the United States or by any State on account of race, color, or previous condition of servitude.

2. The Congress shall have power to enforce this article by appropriate legislation.

AMENDMENT 16 - RATIFIED 2/3/1913.

The Congress shall have power to lay and collect taxes on incomes, from whatever source derived, without apportionment among the several States, and without regard to any census or enumeration.

AMENDMENT 17 - RATIFIED 4/8/1913.

The Senate of the United States shall be composed of two Senators from each State, elected by the people thereof, for six years; and each Senator shall have one vote. The electors in each State shall have the qualifications requisite for electors of the most numerous branch of the State legislatures.

When vacancies happen in the representation of any State in the Senate, the executive authority of such State shall issue writs of election to fill such vacancies: Provided, That the legislature of any State may empower the executive thereof to make temporary appointments until the people fill the vacancies by election as the legislature may direct.

This amendment shall not be so construed as to affect the election or term of any Senator chosen before it becomes valid as part of the Constitution.

AMENDMENT 18 - RATIFIED 1/16/1919. REPEALED BY AMENDMENT 21, 12/5/1933.

1. After one year from the ratification of this article the manufacture, sale, or transportation of intoxicating liquors within, the importation thereof into, or the exportation thereof from the United States and all territory subject to the jurisdiction thereof for beverage purposes is hereby prohibited.

2. The Congress and the several States shall have concurrent power to enforce this article by appropriate legislation.

3. This article shall be inoperative unless it shall have been ratified as an amendment to the Constitution by the legislatures of the several States, as provided in the Constitution, within seven years from the date of the submission hereof to the States by the Congress.

AMENDMENT 19 - RATIFIED 8/18/1920.

The right of citizens of the United States to vote shall not be denied or abridged by the United States or by any State on account of sex.

Congress shall have power to enforce this article by appropriate legislation.

AMENDMENT 20 - RATIFIED 1/23/1933.

1. The terms of the President and Vice President shall end at noon on the 20th day of January, and the terms of Senators and Representatives at noon on the 3d day of January, of the years in which such terms would have ended if this article had not been ratified; and the terms of their successors shall then begin.

2. The Congress shall assemble at least once in every year, and such meeting shall begin at noon on the 3d day of January, unless they shall by law appoint a different day.

3. If, at the time fixed for the beginning of the term of the President, the President elect shall have died, the Vice President elect shall become President. If a President shall not have been chosen before the time fixed for the beginning of his term, or if the President elect shall have failed to qualify, then the Vice President elect shall act as President until a President shall have qualified; and the Congress may by law provide for the case wherein neither a President elect nor a Vice President elect shall have qualified, declaring who shall then act as President, or the manner in which one who is to act shall be selected, and such person shall act accordingly until a President or Vice President shall have qualified.

4. The Congress may by law provide for the case of the death of any of the persons from whom the House of Representatives may choose a President whenever the right of choice shall have devolved upon them, and for the case of the death of any of the persons from whom the Senate may choose a Vice President whenever the right of choice shall have devolved upon them.

5. Sections 1 and 2 shall take effect on the 15th day of October following the ratification of this article.

6. This article shall be inoperative unless it shall have been ratified as an amendment to the Constitution by the legislatures of three-fourths of the several States within seven years from the date of its submission.

AMENDMENT 21 - RATIFIED 12/5/1933.

1. The eighteenth article of amendment to the Constitution of the United States is hereby repealed.

2. The transportation or importation into any State, Territory, or possession of the United States for delivery or use therein of intoxicating liquors, in violation of the laws thereof, is hereby prohibited.

3. The article shall be inoperative unless it shall have been ratified as an amendment to the Constitution by conventions in the several States, as provided in the Constitution, within seven years from the date of the submission hereof to the States by the Congress.

AMENDMENT 22 - RATIFIED 2/27/1951.

1. No person shall be elected to the office of the President more than twice, and no person who has held the office of President, or acted as President, for more

than two years of a term to which some other person was elected President shall be elected to the office of the President more than once. But this Article shall not apply to any person holding the office of President when this Article was proposed by the Congress, and shall not prevent any person who may be holding the office of President, or acting as President, during the term within which this Article becomes operative from holding the office of President or acting as President during the remainder of such term.

2. This article shall be inoperative unless it shall have been ratified as an amendment to the Constitution by the legislatures of three-fourths of the several States within seven years from the date of its submission to the States by the Congress.

AMENDMENT 23 - RATIFIED 3/29/1961.

1. The District constituting the seat of Government of the United States shall appoint in such manner as the Congress may direct: A number of electors of President and Vice President equal to the whole number of Senators and Representatives in Congress to which the District would be entitled if it were a State, but in no event more than the least populous State; they shall be in addition to those appointed by the States, but they shall be considered, for the purposes of the election of President and Vice President, to be electors appointed by a State; and they shall meet in the District and perform such duties as provided by the twelfth article of amendment.

2. The Congress shall have power to enforce this article by appropriate legislation.

AMENDMENT 24 - RATIFIED 1/23/1964.

1. The right of citizens of the United States to vote in any primary or other election for President or Vice President, for electors for President or Vice President, or for Senator or Representative in Congress, shall not be denied or abridged by the United States or any State by reason of failure to pay any poll tax or other tax.

2. The Congress shall have power to enforce this article by appropriate legislation.

AMENDMENT 25 - RATIFIED 2/10/1967.

1. In case of the removal of the President from office or of his death or resignation, the Vice President shall become President.

2. Whenever there is a vacancy in the office of the Vice President, the President shall nominate a Vice President who shall take office upon confirmation by a majority vote of both Houses of Congress.

3. Whenever the President transmits to the President pro tempore of the Senate and the Speaker of the House of Representatives his written declaration that he is unable to discharge the powers and duties of his office, and until he transmits to them a written declaration to the contrary, such powers and duties shall be discharged by the Vice President as Acting President.

4. Whenever the Vice President and a majority of either the principal officers of the executive departments or of such other body as Congress may by law provide,

transmit to the President pro tempore of the Senate and the Speaker of the House of Representatives their written declaration that the President is unable to discharge the powers and duties of his office, the Vice President shall immediately assume the powers and duties of the office as Acting President.

Thereafter, when the President transmits to the President pro tempore of the Senate and the Speaker of the House of Representatives his written declaration that no inability exists, he shall resume the powers and duties of his office unless the Vice President and a majority of either the principal officers of the executive department or of such other body as Congress may by law provide, transmit within four days to the President pro tempore of the Senate and the Speaker of the House of Representatives their written declaration that the President is unable to discharge the powers and duties of his office. Thereupon Congress shall decide the issue, assembling within forty eight hours for that purpose if not in session. If the Congress, within twenty one days after receipt of the latter written declaration, or, if Congress is not in session, within twenty one days after Congress is required to assemble, determines by two thirds vote of both Houses that the President is unable to discharge the powers and duties of his office, the Vice President shall continue to discharge the same as Acting President; otherwise, the President shall resume the powers and duties of his office.

AMENDMENT 26 - RATIFIED 7/1/1971.

1. The right of citizens of the United States, who are eighteen years of age or older, to vote shall not be

denied or abridged by the United States or by any State on account of age.

2. The Congress shall have power to enforce this article by appropriate legislation.

AMENDMENT 27 - RATIFIED 5/7/1992.

No law, varying the compensation for the services of the Senators and Representatives, shall take effect, until an election of Representatives shall have intervened.